Small-Group Discussion
in Orientation
and Teaching

Small-Group Discussion in Orientation and Teaching

by

RANDALL W. HOFFMANN and **ROBERT PLUTCHIK**
Hofstra College

G. P. PUTNAM'S SONS   New York

ACKNOWLEDGMENTS

THE AUTHORS *wish to acknowledge with gratitude the helpful criticisms of Dr. Evelyn Shirk and Dean Esther Kronovet and the patient and painstaking assistance of Mrs. Jeanne Ritter. We also wish to thank our many colleagues at Hofstra College whose work in the Orientation program and whose thoughtful discussion of our philosophy, principles, and method have helped us considerably in clarifying our own thinking.*

Foreword

ALTHOUGH this book describes in detail a new approach to helping students make the most of their college experiences through a new type of orientation course, I suspect—and the authors hope—that its most profound effect may be in helping college professors create college experiences that will make the most of the students!

Commissions of thoughtful educators, some Foundation spokesmen and a few educational prophets are stating ever more positively that simply lecturing at large groups of students in college is not necessarily the best way to educate them. A rising tide of opinion holds that college students must take more responsibility for self-education, must become more critical, must show more intellectual initiative and should become more intellectually excited. Often this thinking relates to the problem of financing the education of the increasing numbers of college students, but usually states squarely that the taking even of copious lecture notes, doing required reading, writing required papers and regurgitating on examinations will not stimulate many students to take initiative, to become critical and creative, and to be self-educating.

But what to do about this problem! Lambasting college

students doesn't solve it; they are looking desperately for help themselves, and finding little. Blaming college teachers usually places them squarely on the defensive and serves to entrench them more deeply in their time-honored, though vulnerable, ruts. Professors Hoffmann and Plutchik would not abandon lectures entirely; on the contrary, they see good use for lectures. They would, however, supplement lectures with other experiences for students, carefully designed to stimulate critical thinking, creativity, initiative, intellectual honesty and excitement, and they describe exactly how these other experiences may be developed.

Orientation courses, not more than 40 years old, have afforded an excellent laboratory in which to discover that students were not greatly affected by being lectured at. They have also provided good grounds for experimentation. Often, thanks to the caution of college faculties, orientation courses, although required of students, have not been loaded down with the impedimenta of credits and grades. This has given opportunity to the more creative in charge of orientation courses to experiment and make bold efforts to accomplish their objectives. From reliance on straight information-giving, accomplished by means of lectures and readings, we have progressed gradually to the position described so clearly in this book.

Quite frankly, one of the obstacles in advancing to this position has been the fact that dividing freshmen into small groups for orientation has required the participation of a considerable number of faculty members. While some faculty have prized the opportunity this presented, have enjoyed it, and have even added it onto the rest of their teaching load, others assigned to this responsibility have felt uncomfortable and at a loss as to what to do when confronted with the relatively unstructured, free situation that most small orientation groups present. Those who have enjoyed working with orientation groups will enoy them increasingly after reading this book. Others who feel some disturbance or even resentment at being saddled with an orientation group may find here not only a life saver, but also a new kind of intellectual challenge.

While the authors are to be congratulated not only on this helpful report of their experimentation, but even more on the skill and understanding with which they have developed their methods over the years, I would raise two questions with them. First, we know from some of the new studies of campus societies that the implicit values, pressures, and interactions are unique and vary strikingly from college to college. We also know that students are immediately and inexorably acted upon by these values, pressures, and interaction systems. Might it be well with the help of social scientists, to sensitize freshmen in orientation courses to the fact that they have now become components in a new and unique kind of society, that they will be acted upon by it, but not only do they not need to "adjust" to it, but they can even modify the system if they choose to do so? Therein, in my view, lie unexplored possibilities.

Second, how about taking on for a second semester (either with or without credit) those who show outstanding interest and ability in studying their college as a social system? Sophomores thus further educated in an understanding of the college that they had met as freshmen could be invaluable in opening the eyes of the innocent in-coming freshmen in orientation groups the following fall. This would have at least two other values: it would provide the start for a strong system of responsible student leadership for campus life and would afford for an interested group an excellent introduction for their future study of community social systems, labor relations, politics, primitive societies—or what have you.

Certainly to call orientation through small-group development a "personnel service," as some experts in personnel work may thoughtlessly do, would be vastly to underestimate the significance of what Professors Hoffmann and Plutchik are describing. This is in reality higher education in some of its more creative aspects.

Esther Lloyd-Jones, Head
Department of Guidance and
Student Personnel Administration
Teachers College, Columbia University

Preface

DURING the past six or seven years the authors of this book have been engaged in developing a freshman orientation course at a liberal arts college enrolling approximately 2800 full-time students. Our study of orientation courses at other colleges and our experience with our own have convinced us that the purposes of orientation are best realized through a small-group approach, with teachers employing a group-centered method of leadership.

This book is written primarily but not exclusively for those who are interested in the problems of freshman orientation. Its prospective readers are faculty engaged in teaching an orientation course and administrative officers directing and developing such a course. Even if they are not committed to the group-centered method, there is much in this book to interest them. If they are committed to the group-centered method, much of the material in this book will be of vital import.

The book is based on the authors' experience and on their reasonably wide study in group-centered theory and practice. Consequently, there is within its pages much actual case material as well as a fairly extensive review of methodology, general principles, and philosophy.

We also hope that this book will be of value to any teacher—college, secondary school, or elementary school—who is interested in small-group discussion as an educational method. The principles and practices enunciated here can be applied to almost any course situation even though the authors have focussed primarily on orientation courses for college freshmen.

Randall W. Hoffmann
Robert Plutchik

Contents

Appendix

Small-Group Discussion
in Orientation
and Teaching

ORIENTATION
PRACTICES AND TRENDS

*Extent of Orientation Courses in American
Colleges and Universities*

ALTHOUGH orientation courses as a formal discipline started as early as 1920, it was not until recent years that they became common enough to be considered an accepted part of the undergraduate curricular pattern. Recent studies show that very nearly half of the colleges and universities in the United States conduct an orientation course of at least one semester's duration for their beginning students.

A. G. Breidenstine, in his report to the Eastern Association of College Deans and Advisers of Men, in November, 1953, indicated that 70% of the Middle Atlantic Colleges had freshman orientation programs, with an average duration of one semester. In a more recent study of sixty-nine small colleges, George H. Greene found that 52.1% had a freshman orientation course, and of those who did not, 36.3% were planning to add one to their freshman curriculum. In a national sampling of 340 colleges (including junior colleges) the authors of the present volume found that 44%

of the colleges and universities of the country have an orientation course of at least one semester.[1]

Despite the prevalence of orientation courses and despite the increasing awareness on the part of educators of the need for such a course, it is evident that there is something short of total agreement concerning the goals, the framework, and the method of teaching it.

Programs such as Orientation Week and periodic orientation lectures during the first semester were originally conceived as an aid to the student in "bridging the gap" between high school and college. When the startling casualty rate among college students and especially the high mortality rate among freshmen became evident to educators (more than a 30% drop-out by the end of the first year), it was seen that stronger measures were needed to help the student adapt to his college environment.

College educators have long been aware, however, that drop-outs are only one example of the considerable human waste that occurs among college students. If a young person does not make the most of his college potential, this also is failure; if a student continues in college with a wrong notion of what college can and should do for him, even though he earns a degree, this too is failure; if a student fails to get the most out of college, whether for reasons of correctable incapacity or because of debilitating attitudes, this too is failure.

It became apparent that the alleviation of these kinds of failure fell within the province of orientation, and so the scope of the course was broadened and its depth increased.

[1] R. Plutchik & R. W. Hoffmann, "The Small-Group College Orientation Program," *Journal of Higher Education*, 1958, 29, 278-279.

Fewer and fewer colleges are content to rely on venerable institutions such as "orientation week" to achieve such broad and important goals. Orientation week may include a great variety of activities: registration, testing, meeting faculty members, meeting student leaders, social events, faculty and administration lectures, giving out of informational materials, and informal group discussions. What the student takes with him from orientation week is hardly measurable, but it can be safely said that he takes far less than the college hopes for.

Strengths and Limitations of Traditional Programs

Various authorities have pointed out the weaknesses in such practices, which criticisms are pretty well summarized by Daniel J. Grier.

> Critical evaluation of these techniques indicates that while many of them are theoretically planned to be of lasting value as functions of deeper teaching, the practice is frequently at variance with the theory. One of the essential weaknesses is that for the most part they concentrate on the first few days and except for some counseling or continuation courses the student is then almost entirely on his own... Much of the information given out during freshman week is in lecture form and the student is on the receiving end of a one-way line with little opportunity to relate the information to his personal adjustment. At the same time this period is often one of considerable confusion, much of the program serves only to further confuse the student, and it is probable that the results are the opposite of those intended. What seems to be ignored is the fact that many adjustment problems do not become real to them until students are well along in college

and that adjustment to the academic program is often the most difficult problem the student faces.[2]

Over the years, however, improvements have been made in the orientation-week programs by eliminating some of the events that serve purely administrative purposes such as registration and the giving of various tests, and substituting small-group discussions for the traditional lectures. This healthy development has been noted and commended by Arbuckle: "If the program during orientation week is to accomplish its purpose of helping the student to feel that he belongs, that he is part of an institution interested in him as an individual, then there must be some opportunity for him to get together with his fellow freshmen, with other students, and with faculty members in small groups." [3]

It would seem then that orientation week can have a meaningful place in helping the student make a propitious start in his college career. It can give him some inkling of the expectations and demands of his new environment, and it can help to make him feel accepted at college. This is a significant start, but even this can be wasted unless there is a follow-up.

The follow-up sometimes takes the form of a series of lectures given during the first semester or over the full year and sometimes is formalized into a full-fledged orientation "course" that may or may not be given semester-hour credit. In a study reported in the December, 1948, issue of *Occu-*

[2] "The New Student Arrives at College," in *Student Personnel Work as Deeper Teaching,* edited by Esther Lloyd-Jones, New York, Harper & Brothers, 1954, p. 50.

[3] D. S. Arbuckle, *Student Personnel Services in Higher Education,* New York, McGraw-Hill, 1953, p. 69.

pations, Gladys Bookman noted that out of 143 colleges, 61 required an orientation course and 12 gave a series of required lectures; 49 gave credit for the course (from one to three hours) and 22 gave no credit. As can be seen from the studies cited earlier in this chapter, the trend is toward formalization of the orientation program into a course resembling in many respects the usual academic courses found in the college curriculum.

There are, however, some basic differences between the orientation course and the traditional academic offerings, as well as variety of methods in administering and teaching it.

In the old days the course was often found under the aegis of one of the academic departments, sometimes the philosophy department, sometimes sociology, sometimes English. This practice seems to be on the way out, for it soon became obvious that the orientation course was too often confused with the subject matter of the department administering it and was ending up as a kind of mongrel philosophy, sociology, or English course.

The commonest practice now is to center the administration of the orientation course in Student Personnel Services, with the Dean of Students or his delegate taking the responsibility for directing its destiny. In this setting it becomes an interdepartmental course, with selected faculty, specialists, visiting lecturers, or even upper-class students taking an active part in the teaching.

A less wide but still significant variation is found in the subject matter of orientation as a course. Some colleges concentrate on academic skills and techniques: how to read, how to study, how to take notes, how to use the library, and so forth. Some colleges spend much time on vocational adjustment, others on personal adjustment, that is, mental health or applied psychology. Still others emphasize adjustment to the social and co-curricular aspects of college, and still others are predominantly concerned with the intellectual and cultural heritage of today's world.

Methods of teaching the course are less varied but are probably the most significant factor in its success or failure. The lecture—either to large or small groups—is the most common technique and the one that seems to produce the least results. As Arbuckle says, ". . . the pattern is sometimes a lecture-dominated type of course where such problems as how to study, how to use the library, how to adjust to college life, and how to prepare for a vocation are discussed. For many freshmen these talks are quite impersonal and have no particular meaning. A discussion of how to use the library, for example, becomes much more meaningful when the students are taking a course in English, where it is necessary to use the library, than when it is merely presented as one of the topics in the course." [4]

Grier and Bookman also think little of the lecture as a means toward the ends of orientation. Grier says, citing Bookman as being in agreement, "Even the continuation programs are largely ineffective . . . since many of the orientation courses are lectures and again the student is at the receiving end only." [5]

New Trends in Orientation

Of the many devices used to orient the freshman to his new environment—devices which include mass lectures,

[4] *Ibid.,* p. 77.
[5] *Op. cit.,* p. 51.

round-table discussions, campus and off-campus tours, audio-visual aids, individual counseling, group counseling, special social events, visits to faculty homes, and any amount of informational and inspirational reading material—the most effective seems to be the small-group discussion run on a "democratic" or group-centered basis.

Grier makes the point that "A number of colleges have experimented with various types of small group orientation with some success and this appears to be one of the most promising trends among orientation techniques." [6] In the 340 college study made by the authors of the present volume, the majority reported conducting their courses on a lecture basis. Many of these confessed, however, that they would much prefer the small-group type of orientation if they could find ways and means of introducing it at their institutions.

From the foregoing, it can be seen that variations among colleges in their treatment of the orientation problem are considerable. A few words remain to be said about the several concepts of the purpose, function, or goal of orientation. Here an apparent agreement turns out to be superficial, with some deep-lying conflicts bubbling under a calm surface unanimity.

Most educators readily agree that an orientation course or program should serve to help the student "adjust" to his new environment, help him "adapt" to the college experience, help him "bridge the gap" between high school and college. This consensus on the word *adjustment,* or something synonymous, does not tell a true story, for interpreta-

[6] *Op. cit.,* p. 57.

tions of the word as applied to a freshman in the college setting are rather varied.

One person may mean by *adjustment* simply the student's familiarity with his physical or geographical surroundings, a more or less complete knowledge of campus facilities. Another may be talking about academic adjustment, an increasing familiarity with the tools of learning, a gradually increasing mastery of academic skills and techniques. Another may be talking about mental health, an inward, personal adjustment, which brings orientation into the realm of therapy. And still others are talking about intellectual adjustment, a process that will make the student feel at home when he rubs shoulders with the giants of literature, science, sociology, and philosophy.

Such variations played on the general theme of adjustment lead inevitably to differences in the final product, the orientation course, since the purpose of any course must to a large extent determine its content and the method used in teaching it.

The Present Conception of Orientation Functions

The remainder of the present chapter will be devoted to resolving to some extent the differences noted above and to delineating as precisely as we can the purpose, aim, or end of an orientation course.

The new freshman on a college campus is undoubtedly in need of a certain amount of information concerning his physical environment before he can begin to function effectively. He has to know where his classrooms are, where certain administrative offices are located, and, as time goes on, a great deal more about the geography of the campus if he is to take advantage of the facilities available to him. The mistake often made, however, is in overestimating the amount of information needed to make a start, with the consequence that the student is deluged with directions that he can neither use nor retain.

A more efficient way of handling the physical environment problem is, first, to assume that if the student really wants such information he will get it providing it is available; secondly, the essential information should be made conveniently available in pamphlet or bulletin form.

Much the same stand can be taken in regard to mastering the tools of learning. If a student really wants to learn how to study, one need do little more for him than to let him know that there is instructional material galore in this area. Even if one feels that a student should receive more careful and stringent direction in improving his study skills, one can hardly expect the orientation course to be very specific in this regard. It is more logical to assume that the best instruction for studying French can be given in the French class, for studying science, in the science class, and for studying mathematics, in the mathematics class. The orientation class can more profitably spend its time in trying to develop healthy attitudes toward the tools of learning and toward the academic courses themselves.

The therapeutic function of orientation courses is not to be dismissed lightly. Opinion is divided on how much emphasis can be and should be put on therapy as a function of orientation. Even an authority such as Arbuckle contradicts himself on this point. On one page he makes the following statement: "If an individual is not adjusted personally, if his emotional stability is such that he cannot withstand shocks and pressures without being overcome, then it would appear to be pointless to try to adjust him specifically to college life, to married life, or to any other 'way' of life." On the next page, in describing an orientation course that he himself directs, he says, "Such a course is therapeutic in nature, and it is basically an attempt to help the student to understand his own behavior as well as the behavior of others." [7]

There can be little doubt that if an orientation course is conducted in such a way that the emphasis is put on the student and his problems in making an adequate adaptation to college, or in other words, in such a way that the student as a person is the focus of attention, then the course will be to some extent therapeutic. The therapy is concomitant and incidental, however, rather than a primary end of the course.

There is far less brief for considering orientation a parade ground on which the student sees pass in review the intellectual giants of the ages. Such a course is undoubtedly valuable, and we wish to cast no reflections on Contemporary Civilization programs, but this is not what is meant by orientation. The purpose of a course such as Contemporary Civilization is to give the student an intellectual experience of considerable breadth and depth, to make him acquainted with some of the best thinking of our culture and others. It is in itself a college education in small. *The purpose of orientation is to help the student become more receptive to such experiences.*

Orientation, then, is not simply an information-giving process, not exclusively a training course in how to use the tools of learning, not primarily therapy nor applied psy-

---

[7] Arbuckle, *op. cit.*, pp. 77-8.

chology, not a survey course in the social sciences, literature, or philosophy.

Little quarrel can be found, we think, with the notion that
the purpose of orientation is, simply, to increase the student's receptivity to the total college experience.

Most college teachers, counselors, and administrators are
aware from long experience that a student's receptivity to
college is not necessarily governed by his potential. Many
students of high potential do not get all that they should out
of college, and many students of average potential get almost
nothing at all. The job of orientation is to increase the student's receptivity to the extent that he will get out of college
all that his potential will allow. Less than this, as we said
earlier, is a form of failure.

Very few students come to college with complete willingness to make the most out of their potential as a thinking
and acting human being, just as very few persons in any
walk of life actually use their resources to the limit. Orientation is a process designed to overcome this reluctance to give
one's all, designed to break down the barriers that stand
between the opportunity that college offers and the ability
of the student to make the most of this opportunity.

What these barriers are specifically—that is, what it is
that blocks a student's receptivity to college—will be discussed in the next chapter. In this, and in later chapters,
when we talk about the methods, techniques, and devices
used in helping the student become more receptive to the
college experience, we will in effect be talking about the
methods, techniques, and devices of the group-centered
process as applied to orientation.

ORIENTATION THROUGH
THE SMALL-GROUP APPROACH
—PHILOSOPHY AND AIMS

The Importance of Attitudes

THE experiences of a freshman at college are undoubtedly colored by the capabilities he brings to the job of being a student. If he is a poor reader, he will find hard sledding in most of his courses; if he is a poor writer, he is due for disappointment and frustration; if he relates inadequately to authority or to his peers, he may well grow inward without growing inwardly. In other words the battle may be feebly fought, or even lost, because of inadequate armament.

Such weaknesses, not at all uncommon, call for remedial action. And it is the policy of some colleges and universities to offer remedial courses in reading, writing, mathematics, and even in etiquette and social behavior. These courses, with their concentration on bringing the student's performance up to par in certain areas, should not be confused with freshman orientation, which has a developmental rather than a remedial function. A student may well take a remedial course in mathematics and thus overcome a serious handicap but at the same time be very much in need of what orientation has to give him.

Orientation is not concerned with any specific area, any

specific weakness. It is concerned with the over-all relation that a student makes to his total college experience. It is concerned with the student's physical, intellectual, and emotional reaction to the college environment. It is concerned with the student as a person relating to a many-dimensional pattern of action, thought, and feeling. It is concerned with making this relationship satisfactory, and by *satisfactory* is meant that it will come as close as possible to tapping his full potential as a developing human being.

Along with certain weaknesses and certain strengths the student brings with him to college a set of attitudes. These attitudes, depending on their nature, can either hinder or help the developmental process that characterizes true education.

All teachers, whether they teach courses in English composition, mathematics, accounting, sociology, economics, or what have you, run head-on into negative or otherwise unproductive attitudes among their students and have found themselves helpless in the face of them. A student may feel that a course in German, required in his chosen curriculum, will be useless to him when he gets out on the job. Or it may be, "I never liked English and I never done very good in it."

Perhaps it is the job of the German teacher and the English teacher to dispel such attitudes first before going on with their subject, but very few teachers have time to spare from the actual teaching of their subject for this fundamental process. As a result, the attitudes persist, and the student fails to give what he should give to the course and fails to get out of it what it is capable of giving him.

But incorrect attitudes toward particular courses are not the only ones that may impede the educational process.

Attitudes in six or seven other areas also play a significant part in the student's progress or lack of progress. They will simply be listed here and dealt with at length later in this chapter.

Attitude toward the purpose of a college education
Attitude toward the tools of learning
Attitude toward authority
Attitude toward peers
Attitude toward parents and family
Attitude toward self

This list is not intended to be exhaustive. There are perhaps other attitudes that for any one individual might be more significant than any of those listed, as, for example, attitude toward sex, or toward vocations, or toward religious experience. The areas mentioned, however, are undoubtedly the ones that are most generally significant in the life of a college student.

It can be argued, and justly, that if a student's attitude in certain of these areas is unhealthy, that is, likely to keep him from getting the most out of college, he should not have been admitted in the first place.

President Butterfield of Wesleyan University has something to say on this point:

> I see no reason why the flood of students should be allowed to pour into college, why automatic graduation from high school should qualify anyone for admission. We ought to recognize, and make people in general recognize, that a desire for economic or social advantage . . . is not enough . . . I think the effort (to educate people with this kind of motive) will result largely in giving more people more bad edu-

cation. As an untutored but shrewd acquaintance of mine put it to me the other day, "Everybody's getting to be a college boy, and each one dumber than the next."

President Butterfield is talking about an attitude, very common indeed, toward the purpose of a college education; he is condemning those persons who think of college solely or primarily in terms of the vocational and social advantage that will accrue to them by virtue of their having a college degree. Said one student, a veteran, "In my three years out of high school I found out that if you're going to get anywhere in today's labor market you've got to have that 'piece of paper,' and I'm here to get it, the sooner the better." This student's motivation for college was strong—but wrong! And Dr. Butterfield would question whether such a student should be admitted to college at all.

No matter how we feel about admitting students with that kind of attitude or similar ones, the fact remains that they are admitted, and by the thousands. If the attitude persists and remains their primary motivation throughout four years of college, they will surely miss a great deal that college has to offer; and, if they manage to meet the minimum requirements in their courses, they will eventually be graduated to join what Dr. Butterfield calls a "host of degree-bearing morons."

Weeding out such students at the admissions stage might prove to be a difficult task indeed unless an infallible test could be devised that would reveal the quality of a prospective student's motivation. Perhaps, also, it is unjust to discriminate against such attitudes when other sectors of our culture tend to encourage and foster them. The colleges would, in effect, be refusing admission to a student who is the victim of his culture instead of accepting him as the product of his culture and doing as good a job as possible with him.

It is also argued, with even more justice, that the changing of damaging attitudes is the job of every teacher with whom a student comes in contact. Thus, if a student's attitude toward English is negative, the English teacher must deal with the attitude as part of the course. If a student feels hostile toward authority, the teacher must do what he can to dispel this hostility. In other words, the student as a human being must come first and the subject matter second.

If this were a universal philosophy in American colleges and if teaching methods could be everywhere adopted that would carry out this philosophy, then there would be little need for a special course or program in orientation. Colleges like Sarah Lawrence, Bennington, Bard, and Antioch, where the educational philosophy and methodology are of this nature, have an orientation process built into every course and college activity. Attitudes, feelings, motivation are never forgotten, dismissed, nor relegated to some non-academic area of the college. Dealing with them in the hope of changing them for the better is one of the primary concerns of teaching and teachers.

But, unfortunately, only a very few American colleges can afford to put this philosophy into action even if they whole-heartedly believe in it. In most colleges, economic pressures dictate large classes, where the lecture, perhaps supplemented by a few audio-visual aids, is the only feasible teaching method, and do not permit much consideration of a student's attitudes, feelings, or motivation, no matter how deeply the teacher may be concerned with the full personal development of the individual student. And so the college and the teacher find it necessary to content themselves with brushing the surface of the student's mind rather than probing for attitudes ingrained and damaging.

What we have been saying, then, is that attitudes are part of the equipment that a student brings to his college experience and that certain negative attitudes keep him from getting as much out of that experience as his potential will allow. We have indicated that this problem probably cannot be solved in the admissions office and that only a very few colleges can deal with it as an integral part of the regular teaching process.

Orientation in Relation to Attitudes

We believe that most colleges and college educators are aware of these facts, have been aware of them for some time, and that orientation courses are, in essence, their answer to the problem.

"This may be all very well," someone may say, "but I've found that the main trouble with students is that they don't know how to study. What are you going to do about that?" Behind the question lies the perfectly legitimate assumption that orientation should teach the student how to study. If students themselves are asked what their biggest trouble is in college, seven times out of ten they will answer that they don't know how to study and have never been taught how. The student, too, may quite logically blame the orientation course for not teaching him how to study. But this reaction is seen to be something less than logical when we find that we get the same answers from students who attended orientation courses in which one quarter of the total time was given to teaching study skills! "Oh, yes," says the student, "I had it in orientation, but somehow I never learned."

In one or two lectures it is possible to give a student most of the information he needs about study skills and methods. Books, pamphlets, articles by the dozen are available on how to study. On formal and informal tests we find students who can recite backward and forward the principles of the "Survey Q3R" method or the "PQRST" method or whatever other method of study they may have been exposed to. And still they do not know how to study.

The key to this anomaly may very well be contained in a little sentence appearing unobtrusively in an essay by John S. Diekhoff called "Schooling for Maturity": "It is not enough to know what justice is; one must also love it." It is not enough either that a student know all there is to know about study skills and methods; he must also love to study. And so once again we are talking about attitudes.

In our discussion of attitudes that are the legitimate concern of orientation, we have talked so far about attitudes toward the purpose of college and attitudes toward one of the tools of learning, study skills. We would like to go on and say a few words about harmful attitudes in several other areas and show how they can impede a student's progress in college.

It is hard to say nowadays what would be an ideally healthy attitude toward authority on the part of young people who are developing into maturity. We do know two things, however: (1) That in the day-by-day business of getting a college education, the student is thrown into con-

stant contact with authority figures of many different kinds
—faculty, administration, parents, some of their classmates,
and the host of intellectual, ethical, and religious authorities
they meet in their books; (2) that a student's attitude toward
these authority figures will either help or hinder his development toward intellectual and emotional maturity.

A common attitude toward authority is one of hostility
either open or veiled. Very few teachers can completely
escape being a target for this attitude—and, usually, through
no fault of their own. The teacher's status as an authority
figure, no matter how "non-authoritarian" he actually may
be, makes him fair game for arrows of hostility that were
probably engendered elsewhere.

There is little need here to explore the origins of hostilities
that the college student—as well as the rest of us—carries
around with him. The interested reader is referred to an
eye-opening book, *The Hostile Mind,* by Dr. Leon J. Saul,
which examines thoughtfully and in detail the roots and
causes of hostility.[1] What we are concerned with here is not
so much the causes as the effects of a hostile attitude toward
authority on a student's academic progress.

It is possible, of course, for a student to "hate the guts" of
a teacher and still get an "A" in the course. It is considerably
more likely, however, that a student who has hostile feelings toward a teacher, no matter what their origin, will reject either consciously or unconsciously what the teacher has
to offer. The rejection may come in the form of "laziness" or
procrastination or "just getting by" or a deliberate "to-hell-
with-it" attitude. Whatever form it takes, it is usually self-

[1] Leon J. Saul, *The Hostile Mind,* New York, Random House, 1956.

defeating and of course it puts at nought the teacher's legitimate aims.

Authority figures other than teachers may also bear the brunt of hostile attitudes—administrative officers, coaches, parents, student officers in co-curricular activities, and even authors of text books. The effects on the student are the same: hostility blocks to some extent his receptivity to the educational experience.

There are, of course, other attitudes toward authority that are almost equally damaging. As prevalent as hostility, if not more so, is the submissive attitude—or, to use a more general and less highly charged term, an attitude of dependence.

The student who is dependent on authority is found almost as frequently among seniors as among freshmen, except in institutions which practice the philosophy that the job of teaching is to make the student independent of the teacher. The dependent student gets very little more than is given him, and he tends to blame the teacher if he is not given what he thinks he ought to get. He is quite happy as long as the instructor makes it clear what is expected of him: how many words he has to write for an essay, exactly what extra books he has to read, precisely what he has to study for the final examination. But if he is left to his own devices, he is likely to feel dreadfully insecure and even resentful.

Such students tend also to become more dependent on the written word than on their own power of thought. They take their opinions from authorities in the field and go no further. If such and such a great man said something on a particular subject, then that is enough for them—they quote him or paraphrase him and close their minds to any other point of view.

The dependent attitude is particularly hard to deal with. For some teachers there is considerable ego satisfaction in a student's dependence. He finds it pleasanter to answer a student's questions than to risk creating resentment by suggesting that the student find the answers for himself; he prefers to hand out capsules of pre-digested knowledge to having the student graze for himself; he finds it more satisfying, and easier, to be continually in the giving role than to adopt the role of stimulator of a student's self-education.

And so attitudes of dependence are quite often nourished rather than discouraged, with the consequence that the student fails to appreciate or trust the power of his own mind; his education becomes limited to the things he has been told by his teacher and the books he has been told to read. In a word, he has not achieved an education in the full sense of the word; that is, he has not been oriented toward the life-long process which is self-education.

An attitude toward authority, then, that is marked by hostility or overdependence can limit a student's receptivity to various parts of the college experience. If he is going to make the most out of himself and the most out of college, such attitudes must change.

In addition to the attitudes we have so far discussed, a student's attitude toward himself may also make a considerable difference in his educability, his ability to assimilate knowledge or achieve insight.

In students' comments about what freshman orientation with group-centered leadership has done for them, we have found that the most common expression of appreciation runs somewhat like this: "From group discussion one learns that the problems confronting him are faced by others. He ceases to feel sorry for himself, and difficulties fall into perspective." (Actually, this is a verbatim quotation from an anonymous evaluation.) Judging from the frequency of this kind of comment, one can assume that a great many freshmen start college and continue with the attitude that their problems are unique. This attitude, as the student quoted above points out, distorts their perspective and makes them put too much emphasis on their problems and think too much about themselves to the detriment of the educational process.

Another common reaction to group-centered orientation is the observation, with overtones of surprise, that one can listen without endangering one's integrity to other people's opinion, and one may even find some of these opinions as acceptable as one's own. "Sometimes," says one student, "you may find that you have been wrong about something or you may not have had any opinion on a certain thing and leave a particular discussion with formulated ideas." Or to quote another, "I was impressed by the different viewpoints that one topic has, more specifically, the many different ideas that a number of people may have about one thing."

So common are expressions such as these that one is justified in concluding that the normal freshman comes to college with pretty set opinions and an attitude of obstinacy and rigidity concerning them. Until this attitude is changed, until he learns to respect the opinions of others and to hold his own open to change, part of the educational process is wasted. It should be noted, of course, that respect for another's opinion does not necessarily mean acceptance of it as one's own.

The educational process is impeded by other incorrect attitudes that the student may have toward himself. He may doubt his own self-worth. He may feel incompetent or insecure. He may feel unaccepted. His aspirations or ambitions may be ill-founded in reality. It is the job of orientation to help change such attitudes.

The basic aim of orientation, then, is to modify attitudes in such a way as to help the student become more receptive to what college offers. There are, however, more specific aims or goals, which might be thought of as avenues to the main goal or, to change the figure, as building blocks for the main structure. In the remainder of this chapter we will describe some of the subgoals that are associated with the general aim described above.

The specific areas of change and concern in orientation may be described in the following terms:

1. *The Place of Education in Life.* Through discussion, readings, and sharing of opinions, the students come gradually to a more realistic assessment of the place of a college education in their own lives. They begin to realize that college can not only prepare them for a good job but for a good life as well. Even the meaning of life itself becomes an appropriate subject for discussion.

In a sense, the specialization that is so typical of our colleges is a reflection of the diversity of interests (one might almost say fragmentation) in our society. A course such as orientation, has, as one of its aims, the bringing together for examination of some of the many areas of concern in our lives.

2. *Increased Social Awareness.* Little by little, as the students exchange views on the problems of concern to them they begin to discover that there are many different ways of looking at a problem and that the "facts" which one person takes for granted are unknown to or even challenged by another. Thus a broadening social awareness develops. The conflict of ideas presented openly and seriously is often a stimulus for the development of new syntheses, new integrations which become meaningful in the individual's life. "Knowledge affects behavior in the degree to which the individual has discovered the personal meaning of an idea for him." In fact the fundamental task of education, in the view of Dr. Arthur Combs, is "to assist students to discover for their own behavior the personal meaning of the accumulated culture of our race." [2] Orientation, in an intense, personal way, provides the opportunity for each person to see alternate ways of looking at various social problems.

3. *Increased Self-knowledge.* Although self-knowledge is not the major focus of the orientation group, it often develops through the give and take of discussion. A student may silently listen to a description of some personal experience or reaction of another group member and suddenly see his own behavior in a new light. Such insights are sometimes discussed in individual conference with the orientation teacher; sometimes they are mentioned in the group. Sometimes they remain part of the private world of the person.

4. *Increased Self-confidence.* The development of self-confidence in an individual is generally a function of how successful he is in accomplishing his various objectives and

[2] *The Psychology of the College Student,* The Thorn Lectures, Hofstra College, 1954.

in solving problems as they arise. In the small-group orientation class, many students, for the first time in an academic
setting, discover that their opinions and observations are
listened to with respect and taken seriously. Many students
report that orientation has helped them feel more secure
about asking questions or presenting views in groups, and,
in fact, they often indicate some transfer of this behavior to
their other classes. Since many contacts in life require group
participation the increased self-confidence gained in orientation has much personal value and significance.

5. *Development of Leadership Skills.* There is increasing evidence that in our society, which is dedicated to the
proposition of voluntary cooperation, the concept of leadership is undergoing a certain transformation. Leadership is
beginning to be thought of, not as being invested in one
particular outstanding individual, but as a function which
may be shared by all members of a group. Any member of
the group may initiate new topics, present his opinion, encourage participation by others, mediate disputes, suggest
compromises, or keep discussion moving on subjects under
consideration. Not all of these functions need be performed
by the same person. The responsibility for effective group
discussion or planning must be shared by everyone in the
group, since everyone can contribute to or detract from the
group's progress. In a democratic group, as in a democratic
society, each individual has the right, the opportunity, *and
the responsibility* of presenting his own ideas and defending
his own values. This experience becomes part of one's training for social leadership.

Another aspect of this matter of training for social leadership concerns the role of the orientation teacher. If he in his

own behavior exemplifies these leadership functions, then it becomes relatively easier for the student to identify and desire to use such leadership skills. Democratic leadership is based on the axiom that no one "leader" or individual has a monopoly on good ideas and that the best decisions and deepest insights can occur only when a group learns to use all the resources and experiences at its disposal.

6. *The Improvement of Academic Skills.* Although many college orientation programs tend to consider improvement of academic skills as primary, we believe it to be but one among several other and perhaps more important aims. As noted previously, we believe that for students who really want to learn how to study, a course in How-To-Study is beneficial. For those who do not care, it is virtually useless.[3] The basic problem is the problem of motivation, and correct motivation can be affected much more satisfactorily by attainment of the other goals that have been described than by a frontal assault on specific technical shortcomings of each student. When a student begins to see clearly the place of education in his own life, when he begins to develop increased social awareness, when he develops greater self-knowledge, self-confidence, and leadership skills, the problem of study skills will be taken in stride, for he will then have the desire to achieve these skills.

7. *The Awareness of College Facilities.* Another aim frequently considered part of a college orientation program is to equip each student with a respect for college traditions

---

[3] See M. E. Tresselt, "The How To Study Course," *The Journal of Psychology* 1952, *34,* 31-35. See also R. Plutchik and E. Kronovet "What Is Your Study Quotient?" in *Controversy,* G. P. Putnam's Sons, New York, 1959.

and rules and a knowledge of its buildings and services. Although this is of some importance, it cannot be considered of prime relevance in an orientation course. Such information, *if the student wants it,* is usually readily available in handbooks, brochures, catalogs, guides, or from upper classmen or faculty members. What is important is that the student learn to get such specific information for himself, that his teachers use this opportunity to encourage independent action on the part of the student. Orientation should be devoted primarily to those issues and problems in which group interaction is of maximum relevance to personal development.

Chapter	THE JOB OF THE
	SMALL-GROUP LEADER: GROUP
3.	ATMOSPHERE OR CLIMATE

LEADING a small group toward learning or problem solving or the achievement of insight is not a passive business. The leader has much to do. He cannot expect to withdraw from the group and allow it to take its own course; this is certainly not what is meant by democratic or group-centered leadership. He has to be in there working all the time: working against frustration, working against loss of objectivity, working to understand, to empathize, working to help the group realize its potential for helping the individual and working to help the individual to realize his potential within the group.

He has two main jobs: (1) to establish an atmosphere or climate within the group that will be conducive to individual participation, and (2) through various activities, techniques, and devices to help the individuals and the group to achieve their maximum power.

When fifteen to eighteen persons are meeting for the first time with an established leader, the group atmosphere is likely to be almost tangibly stiff and to inhibit free expression of thought and feeling. Although positive feelings such as curiosity, interest, alertness may be present, there are frequently detectable signs of suspicion, fear, hostility, and other negative attitudes that will have to be dispelled before the group atmosphere will tolerate open discussion.

In the beginning, the group leader is almost exclusively responsible for any change in climate, and he must effect these changes through his own attitudes and his own actions.

He can initiate certain mechanical processes or arrangements that will help to change the group climate for the better. The conventional seating arrangement, for one thing, with the class all facing the teacher, is not ideal for group discussion; a circular arrangement is to be preferred or a round-table, square-table, or rectangular-table arrangement. The leader takes a place that has no special distinction and makes himself physically a part of the group. In addition, he may introduce some sort of device that will help the members learn and remember one another's name.

These simple mechanics—the circular seating arrangement, the leader's non-distinctive position, the communication of names—are not to be thought of as "gimmicks." They are functional; they are designed to facilitate communication, and in so doing they help to create an atmosphere in which there is freedom to express thought, opinion, and feeling.

But physical arrangements alone will not create the desired atmosphere. A second and much more important avenue to a desirable group climate is via the leader's attitudes. Broadly speaking, there are four aspects or characteristics of a good group-centered leader's attitudes. So important are these in establishing the climate of the group that each will be described in detail. These attitudes, of course, represent ideals and, unfortunately, are seldom completely achieved.

Acceptance

From the good group leader will emanate an impression of acceptance of other people, of everyone and anyone in the group. Rarely, if ever, does he verbally declare his acceptance, but his attitude declares itself in ways that are stronger than words.

In speaking of acceptance one cannot emphasize too strongly that we are speaking of an attitude on the part of the leader, his point of view toward other human beings, his way of dealing with individuals, his philosophy, perhaps, of human relations. Dr. Thomas Gordon, in speaking of the "nonthreatening, accepting psychological climate [that the] group-centered leader tries to create for his group," maintains that, "This aim is rooted firmly in his belief that the individual, when free from forces which he perceives as threats to the self or the self-concept, will actualize the positive and constructive forces that are within him." [1] The group-centered leader's acceptance of others, then, is not just a gesture, a device, a technique; it stems from a genuine belief that others are worthy of acceptance, that every individual has within him that which justifies acceptance.

He further believes that acceptance by the leader will help free the individual to be himself, and the "himself" in every case is a worthwhile individual.

Much more could be said, of course, about the philosophy behind a leader's acceptant behavior toward other individuals. Suffice it to say for our present purposes that a group leader is most likely to be successful if his actions, words,

[1] "Group-Centered Leadership and Administration," in Carl R. Rogers, *Client-Centered Therapy,* Houghton Mifflin Co., Boston, 1951, p. 347.

and demeanor are a true reflection of a fundamental belief in the essential goodness of the individual, a mirror of his acceptant attitude toward others.

How, specifically, does a group leader convey acceptance? Generally speaking, and as pointed out above, acceptance is communicated through the leader's actions, words, and expression. But we must remember that expressions and actions can be negative as well as positive. An expression of disbelief, for example, or of scorn or distaste may reveal to an individual in the group, as well as to the group as a whole, that his words are not being accepted; and he may very well go on to the conclusion that he himself is not being accepted. If the leader, to use another example, turns his attention from the group—let's say by looking out the window or reading a book or speaking to a passerby—this action communicates just as plainly as words that the leader is at least momentarily non-acceptant.

The leader's actions and demeanor ought to indicate that he is giving his utmost attention to the group, that he is striving earnestly and sincerely to understand everything that is being said and felt by the group. If he has negative feelings about the group or any individual in it, he should hide them. Of course, if he has reached the limit of his acceptance he may find it impossible not to communicate this to the group. This would mean that he has failed for the moment in one phase of the job of group-centered leadership.

Actions and expressions, then, readily convey either acceptance or nonacceptance on the part of the leader. Words, however, are the chief means of communicating an attitude.

The leader, it is true, talks less than most others in the group, but what he says usually has considerably more significance to the other members in the group and therefore a great deal more influence in establishing the group climate. If he is to succeed in conveying acceptance, the leader must weigh his statements carefully.

Four general rules may serve as a guide:

(1) In speaking to the group or an individual member, be non-judgemental. Avoid, in other words, as much as possible the tendency to evaluate the thought or feeling expressed or to evaluate the person himself.

This is not easy. Our response to almost any statement that others make tends toward evaluation. "You are right. You are wrong. This is good, this bad" are statements of judgement and convey nonacceptance. Yes, they convey nonacceptance even when the response is one of approval, for we must remember that a leader's approval of one person's statement may automatically reject that of someone else in the group who thinks differently. In the long run, evaluative responses, either positive or negative, tend to communicate nonacceptance.

There will be the objection from many persons that evaluation is a good thing, that we spend our lives learning to evaluate situations, persons, and statements. Why, then, are we now being asked to suspend this vital function? We, too, believe that learning to evaluate and to use one's judgement is very important; but we nevertheless ask the leader to suspend the evaluative function. (Remember we are talking about the leader only, not other members of the group.)

In the first place, evaluation of another person's statement tends to block communication.[2] An evaluation by the leader tends to classify the statement in the leader's mind, to categorize it, cubbyhole it, put it away without further thought. "This is good," says the leader, and no further thought is necessary either by the leader, the group, or the originator of the statement. "This is bad," says the leader, and again the judgement closes off thought. If a judgement is positive, the originator of the statement will quite often stop thinking about it; he has had his reward and can relax. If it is negative, the rebuff may close off his thought or it may cause him to respond emotionally, defensively. In either case, objectivity is sacrificed and communication stops.

Evaluation by the group leader tends to prevent members of the group from using their own judgement. If a group member comes to expect an immediate evaluation of his thought by the leader, he tends to neglect the evaluative process himself. In other words, he forms a dependency relationship that eventually defeats the self-educative process.

"But," a reader may ask, "how can a group leader break himself of the habit of making evaluative statements?" A group leader, like anyone else, reacts intellectually and emotionally to statements, actions, or expressions of others. It is not easy for everyone, but certainly it is possible, to learn to contain this reaction and to suppress expression of it if it is evaluative. Secondly, he can train his mind to react descriptively rather than with a judgement. Instead of thinking of a statement as good or bad, he can think of it as describing the speaker's feelings or state of mind: this person feels doubtful or this person feels insecure, or this person's feel-

[2] See Carl R. Rogers, "Barriers and Gateways to Communication," *Harvard Business Review*, July-August, 1952, Vol. 30, pp. 46-52.

ings have been hurt. The leader will not give voice to these thoughts; he is merely training himself to *understand* rather than to judge. When he has achieved this state of grace he will rarely be tempted to make a response that is evaluative and thus communicative of nonacceptance.

Finally, he can force himself to respond "reflectively," that is, in a manner that will reflect the thought or feeling expressed by the speaker. This technique will be enlarged upon later. Simply stated, however, it is the application of a rule stated by Rogers in "Barriers and Gateways to Communication": "Each person can speak up for himself only *after* he has first restated the ideas and feelings of the previous speaker accurately and to that speaker's satisfaction." [3]

(2) The second general rule for conveying acceptance is to appear to give equal attention and weight to every statement no matter what the nature of the statement or who makes it. Not by word nor gesture nor expression should the group leader dismiss one statement as less important than another, or accept a statement as more important than another. If a group member makes a wisecrack, his wisecrack should be accepted by the leader with the same respect that he accepts another's profundity. Otherwise he has failed to accept the "wiseguy," (who probably needs acceptance more than most of the others) and consequently has failed to free him from the need that led to the wisecrack in the first place.

(3) Occasionally the leader will find it necessary to call the attention of the group to existing limits. (The problem of limits will be taken up in more detail later.) Although he

[3] *Ibid.*

must let the group members know that his acceptance of them is unconditional, he must at the same time make them aware of whatever limits there may be on their group activity.

Groups are seldom without limits imposed on them by some kind of outside supervision. Freshman orientation classes, for example, have limits imposed on them by time and length of meeting, insistence upon attendance and punctuality, pre-selection of discussion topics, smoking regulations, and so on. The group works within such limits, and the leader accepts them as part of the framework of operation. But he can continue to convey acceptance of the group by making it clear that the existing limits are part of the framework into which he and the group have contractually entered and do not exist at his caprice. If the group objects to the limits or questions them, he may accept the objections as legitimate topics of discussion but makes it clear that he has no essential control over them.

(4) Finally, one conveys acceptance to the group and the individual by avoiding preaching, advising, or moralizing. This, of course, may seem a heresy to the conventional teacher or "leader-centered" leader. But there is considerable logic in the stricture to avoid such practices, for they imply that the group members are not acceptable as they are. Thus we convey nonacceptance, even though our intentions are perfectly laudable.

One additional word: even the giving of information may at times convey nonacceptance. There may be times when information-giving by the leader is appropriate, but he should remember that such a procedure may very well alter the acceptant climate he has built up in the group. The dangers have been well expressed by Thomas Gordon:

> A leader may convey lack of acceptance simply by giving information. This is especially true when the information has not been asked for, but may also be true when the information has been openly requested. Much depends, of course, upon the leader's own attitude and his manner of giving information. As each of us knows, a person who gives us the impression of "knowing it all" or being "positively correct" will make us bristle up and become for the moment defensive. By his own manner of informing others, he devaluates their worth. He conveys, "I know, but you do not; my way of thinking is correct, yours is not." Lack of acceptance may be conveyed, though to a lesser degree, even when a leader's manner of giving information is not so extremely dogmatic. People tend to resent "being told," even when the informer genuinely has their interest in mind.[4]

Permissiveness

We have talked at some length about acceptance as a characteristic attitude of the group-centered leader and how acceptance is communicated to the group and thus established as part of the group climate. A second desirable quality is an aura of permissiveness.

Permissiveness is a much misunderstood word, and the misunderstandings have led to abuses in the field of progressive education as well as to unjust criticisms of the democratic method of conducting classes and other groups.

Permissiveness does not mean *laissez-faire;* it does not mean that the leader sits by without interest or involvement

---

[4] T. Gordon, *Group-Centered Leadership,* New York, Houghton Mifflin Company, 1955, p. 185.

while the group does whatever it pleases. It does not mean complete freedom for the individual to do whatever comes into his head. It does not mean complete disregard of any pre-arranged purpose that the group may have had. All this would seem too obvious to mention; yet, unfortunately, there actually are some would-be group-centered leaders who do so misinterpret the concept of permissiveness. What such leaders understand as the democratic or group-centered method could better be described as the *laissez-faire* (or perhaps anarchical) method, which is a far cry from what we are talking about in this book.

Another extreme of misunderstanding occurs at the other end of the scale. Some persons in leadership positions adopt the mannerisms of the democratic method and use them as a veneer for essentially autocratic practices. In such cases the identical terms used by group-centered theorists are used to describe leader activities that are far from group-centered. As Gordon puts it:

> Many theories emphasize that the leader must be permissive, yet some of the descriptions of the role of the "permissive" leader sanction such things as checking over-aggressive participants, drawing in non-participants by skillful questions or reassurance, placing some members under personal attack in order to get emotional involvement, sidetracking irrelevancies, and so on. To other leadership theorists, and to us, these behaviors as part of the leader's role would seem far from permissive. . . .[5]

Permissiveness implies a willingness on the part of the leader to have every individual in the group express any fact,

[5] *Ibid.*, p. 160.

feeling, or opinion he may wish to. It implies also, however, freedom for the individual to remain silent, to be, whenever he wishes, a nonparticipant.

When the group climate is characterized by permissiveness, then, there is a feeling of freedom on the part of each individual to involve himself as little or as much as he wishes in the activities of the group. If he wishes to remain a passive listener, he should feel free to do so. And he should have no fear of expressing his thoughts or feelings, even such "dangerous" ones as criticism of the leader, the group, or the institution under whose auspices the group is operating.

Permissiveness, as we have said, exists within limits. A freshman orientation class has limits imposed on it by the college authorities and school regulations, by the general plan of the course, (tests, papers, discussion topics, text, outside readings), and by the fact that the students are not very far advanced academically. The group may impose additional limits on itself, as for example deciding not to talk about religion or deciding not to smoke even though smoking may be otherwise permitted. Finally, the leader may impose additional limits or not, depending on how comfortable he feels in the structure that is already prescribed.

All leaders must operate within certain prescribed limits. These are the reality factors in the situation. It is true that some leaders are in situations where there are very few limits, as in the case of the group therapist. Other leaders must work in situations where there are many limits, as must the foreman in an industrial organization. The group-centered leader, then, is always accepting and permissive *within limits,* but because of his faith in the group's own capacities he sets fewer limits than the leader who basically trusts only himself. Furthermore, the group-centered leader tries to be clear in his own mind about what limits he must set in order to feel secure enough to be accepting of the group. Having much more faith in the potentialities of his group, he is much less inclined to feel pressures on himself from his own superiors and thus translate these into limits for his group.[6]

It should be noted that limits imposed on itself by the group can be changed by the group. Limits imposed by the leader can be changed by the leader. But limits prescribed from outside the group are best looked on by the group and by the leader as unchangeable, although they may be fit topics for discussion.

Warmth or Friendliness

The atmosphere of a group should reflect an attitude of acceptance and permissiveness on the part of the leader. It should also reflect an attitude of warmth and friendliness.

This notion probably needs little development except for one or two cautionary remarks. The leader should be careful not to show more friendliness toward one individual than toward another. His philosophy should include the precept that all group members must be encouraged to feel they are equally deserving of his respect and affection, and he must take pains therefore to distribute his attentions equally. It may well be that the group member who is the least attractive to the leader personally, is most in need of the leader's friendliness and affection.

[6] *Client-Centered Therapy, op. cit.,* p. 356.

Friendliness does not mean a "buddy-buddy" relationship, at least not in a freshman orientation class, where it might well be looked upon by the freshmen themselves with distaste, and suspicion. We have found that our students feel most comfortable when they address the instructor by his title and last name. On the other hand, the use of first names among the group members themselves and by the leader when addressing the group members seems to promote a warm and comfortable atmosphere.

Objectivity

Objectivity as part of the group atmosphere is not easy to achieve. Nevertheless it is an extremely important attitude for the leader to cultivate in himself.

Gradually, as time goes by, an emotional climate may be created that permits group members to respond with objectivity even to direct or tangential attacks on their own biases, vested interests, or objects, persons, or ideas with which they may be deeply involved emotionally. Unfortunately, this kind of objectivity is rare in the group as a whole, but it is absolutely essential to the proper functioning of a good group-centered leader.

When attacks are made on a leader's pet biases, on his leadership, on anything he loves or respects, he should be able to withhold all response, or, if he must respond at all, he should do so in neutral tones and neutral words. Responding in kind, or defensively, or argumentatively, or punitively will do injury to the atmosphere he is trying to create, will blur the image of democratic authority figure he is trying to foster, and will probably do little or no good for the individual who has offended him.

We realize that maintaining always an objective attitude is asking a lot of the leader, more perhaps than he is willing to give, especially if he is accustomed to speaking up loud and clear for his subject (and his biases) in his other classroom teaching. Nevertheless, the group leader will find that if he allows himself to react non-objectively to unpalatable assertions by individuals in the group, the discussion will generally deteriorate into argument, usually with emotional overtones, and the group will be the loser in terms of progress toward its goals.

In describing group atmosphere or climate we have pointed out that a group-centered leader's attitudes are most influential in creating an ideal climate and that the most important attitudes he must foster in himself are acceptance, permissiveness, warmth or friendliness, and objectivity.

It remains only to be said that as the group develops, these attitudes come to be reflected in the group as a whole, and become characteristic of it. At that point it can be said that the group is an acceptant, permissive, warm and friendly, and objective one.

Members of a group, it has often been noted, tend to imitate the attitudes of their leaders. "We are convinced," says Gordon, "that *when the leader brings acceptance to the group, there is a gradual taking-over of this function by the group members.* They become more accepting of each other, they become more tolerant of differences among themselves and they begin to help each other to feel that their contributions, not just those of the leader, are welcome and will be accepted. Consequently, it becomes easier for the members to express their own real attitudes and feelings and to accept the same in others." [7]

Good leader attitudes — acceptance, permissiveness, friendliness, and objectivity, which in turn establish a satisfactory group climate, require time, thought, and training for their achievement. The satisfactions, however, are indeed worth the effort.

[7] *Client-Centered Therapy, op. cit.,* p. 357.

THE JOB OF THE
SMALL-GROUP LEADER:
ACTIVITIES AND TECHNIQUES

WE have mentioned before that the group-centered leader's job is not a passive one. The purpose of this chapter is to name and explain the activities that the leader engages in, most of them verbal, in his efforts to help the group realize its potential. The order in which they are taken up are not necessarily indicative of their importance nor of their chronological occurrence in the life of a group.

Goal Setting

Sometime in the early life of the group, and at recurrent periods thereafter, it will become aware of a need to set and/or recognize its goals. The leader should be aware of the desirability of the group's being clear on what its goals are, and he should make it possible for the group to take its goals under consideration.

In an informal, structureless group the need makes itself known by such remarks as, "Well, now that we're all together, where do we go from here"; or "Somebody said this was going to be a discussion group—what do we discuss?" In an orientation class, however, there would normally be a synopsis or a statement of purpose that would give the class a pretty broad clue to its reason for being. (See Appendix for a typical synopsis.) Such synopsis might very well include a list of the main topics that the class is to discuss.

When such a listing occurs the class should periodically have an opportunity to decide the order in which topics will be taken up. This activity, which can include discussion of the relative merits of topics and may also include a "buzz session" to help the group reach a decision, might be thought of as the setting of short-term goals. The activity is initiated by questions such as these being posed by the group or the leader: "What do we do next time?" or "What's the next topic we ought to talk about?"

Somewhere along the line, however, comes the consideration of long-term goals. In our opinion it is best for this question to be initiated by the group, and in our experience it rarely occurs spontaneously in the first few meetings. Orientation classes seem content to go along with "surface" goals at first, apparently feeling that their job is to discuss certain topics and do certain reading that will help them adjust to college. Around the fourth or fifth week of the course, however, sometimes as an expression of dissatisfaction with the group's progress, a more searching examination of goals is likely to be initiated.

Usually the discussion will be triggered by some such question as this: "What are we *really* supposed to be getting out of this course?" or, "It seems to me that we do a lot of talking in this class but never reach any conclusions. Aren't we supposed to decide something once in a while?"

The experienced leader, instead of feeling threatened by such questions, will welcome them as a perfect opening for the class to discuss its goals, and he will try to keep the question open while the group plunges into an examination in depth of its goals. If the group has gone well during the early weeks of the course and the leader has done a passable job, he will be much gratified by the insight the class will show in its recognition of the *real* goals of orientation as discussed in an earlier chapter of this book.

Integration

In the early discussions of the group the integrative function of the leader is usually called upon more extensively than any other of his functions. As the group develops, however, and becomes more experienced, the individual members learn better how to *speak to the point,* and the leader has less worry about whether the group sees an individual's contribution in its relationship to the topic under discussion.

This is essentially the purpose of the integrative function: to point up the relationship of seemingly disparate remarks and to show what bearing a particular statement has on the total discussion. As integrator, the leader helps a speaker "make his point."

Sometimes the talk of a group will seem superficial, wandering, uncoordinated. This apparent aimlessness can be stemmed and the contributions of the group brought to focus by gathering the sense of the remarks under one heading and relating subsequent contributions to this heading. It is very rare for one person to make a remark and then another person in the group to follow it with a statement that is completely unrelated. The leader's job is to see the relatedness and to make the integration.

> Paul: I feel the best reason for going to college is to be able to make more money when you get out.

Bill: I read the other day that the college graduate can expect to make about a hundred thousand dollars more than the non-college graduate during his lifetime.

Joe: There's a good job waiting for me as soon as I get my degree and leave college.

Leader: All of you then, see the purpose of college as an economic one. You seem to be motivated by financial gain.

Such a statement would help the group to know what it is talking about, and from there can follow a discussion of the purposes of college.

Integration, then, is a way of helping the group discussion achieve coherence and unity. The leader tries to tie one statement to another and, in turn, all statements to the single unit of discussion. Gordon calls it the "linking" function.

> The "linking" function of the group-centered leader is related closely to his function of understanding meanings and intents. This is because the meaning or the intent of a member's comment often *is* the link to the main stream of thought or to the previous comments. Its actual linkage is frequently hidden by the content of the comment. Thus, by clarifying the meaning or intent of a comment, the group-centered leader makes clear to the group how the new contribution is related to previous discussion.[1]

Reflection

It has sometimes been said that the group-centered leader has to perform the function of a mirror for the individual

---

[1] *Client-Centered Therapy, op. cit.,* p. 359.

members of the group and for the group as a whole. From this analogy has come the word "reflection" to describe the procedure a leader uses in catching the intellectual content of statement and holding it up for the speaker and the group to perceive, or in catching the emotive tenor of a remark and verbalizing it for purposes of group contemplation. This process keeps discussion open and helps to facilitate communication of fact, opinion, or feeling.

In reflecting intellectual content of a statement the leader may merely repeat the words of the speaker, or he may rephrase the remark, or he may catch the essential meaning and put it in his own words. (As a general rule it is important for him to go no further or deeper than the original speaker has gone, lest by habitually going beyond the group he makes the group dependent on him for its intellectual progress.) Following is an example:

Joe: When I talk to my mother I can't seem to make her see my point of view.

Leader: You can't get your point of view across to your mother.

or

You can't seem to communicate with your mother.

or

You feel pretty frustrated about this business of communicating with your mother.

The last response might be most appropriate if the speaker's tone of voice indicated a fairly strong feeling about the problem.

Questions sometimes call for reflection rather than for any other kind of response. For example, how does one respond to a question like this from a student in an orientation class? "What are you going to do about a teacher that won't even listen to you when you try to tell him why you were absent? Even if you were sick he won't even listen to you. What are you going to do about a teacher like that?" Probably one should not try to answer such a question, not because there isn't any answer but because a recommendation of anything short of violence would probably not be accepted. There is too much antipathetic feeling in the way. The job of the leader, therefore, would be to recognize and reflect the feeling with a response somewhat like this: "You feel pretty upset about that teacher," or "That teacher's giving you a lot of trouble, I gather." The student may go on from there to talk about the situation and express his feelings quite freely and, getting a receptive ear from the leader and the group, will perhaps come around to a constructive answer of his own.

Deflection

Just how much a group leader should allow himself to be used as an information giver or question-answerer is hard to state categorically. It can be safely said, however, that the main job of the group-centered leader, very generally speaking, is gradually to make the group independent of him. Any behavior (such as habitually answering questions or giving information) that increases rather than decreases the group's dependence on the leader is best avoided. Questions asked directly of the leader can be avoided by *deflection*, by putting the question to the group or even right back to the individual.

Joe: What's the best way to get on the college newspaper?

Leader: Do you have any suggestions, Joe?

or

Does the group have any suggestions?

or

Maybe two or three of you would like to investigate that problem.

This is really a process of shrugging off a burden that students have come to expect the teacher to shoulder, and gradually bringing them to a state where they will do their own thinking and their own information getting. Deflection accepts the question as pertinent but shifts the responsibility for the answer from the teacher to the group or back to the questioner.

Initiating

Because of the dependence on authority figures that is typical of students, it takes a long time for a leader to get the group out of the habit of depending on him to initiate discussion, action, or the use of special devices. In time a group ideally becomes pretty much self propelling, which indicates that the leader has gradually shifted the initiating function from himself to the group. In the meantime, however, he will usually find that he is the one who has to say at the beginning of the meeting, "Well, where did we leave off last time?" or "What's on the docket for today?" He will be the one, probably, who has to suggest that a "buzz" session might help the group or that role-playing a particular problem might cast some light on it. He may have to suggest that a committee might like to investigate a particular project and bring a report back to the class. Or he may suggest that it is time the group took a critical, evaluative look at itself.

Before resorting to his initiating function the leader should be sure he has given the group every opportunity to be first with the suggestion. When he does initiate, he must beware of being too forceful should his own suggestion seem to fall on unfertile ground.

Resource

The education and experience of a college instructor may be brought to bear on a problem so that the group will be advanced toward a problem's solution. There is a time, of course, to speak and a time to remain silent, and the leader must judge whether his contribution will advance the solution without retarding the group process. Although he must not allow himself to be used as a crutch, he can sometimes untie a knotty tangle by calling upon his specialized knowledge. A studied reluctance to use his own special knowledge and his own storehouse of facts is probably the best attitude to adopt, at least until he is sure that the group is reasonably independent of him. Faced with such an attitude, the group will tend to exhaust its own facilities and thus be more receptive to the leader's help when such aid is really necessary.

Summary

There are at least two schools of thought concerning a summary at the end of a meeting: one school maintains that a summing up tends to close off thought, that the better practice is to leave the discussion open ended, the loose ends untied, so that the individuals of the group will go on thinking about the subject after the meeting is over; the other school feels that a summarization helps the group look back

over the ground it has traveled and gives it a feeling of satisfaction, a sense of accomplishment. Whether a leader sides
with one school or the other with regard to end-of-meeting
summaries, he will probably find that at some points during
the course of a discussion it becomes appropriate to summarize, especially if the summarization will lead the group
on to a new phase of the subject or make obvious an unexplored area in the phase under consideration. Good results are often achieved by leaving the summary open
ended, *i.e.,* by ending it with a question or with a suggestion
that there may be something the group would like to add.

Clarification

If a statement by an individual is vague or too compli-
cated, it may helpful for the leader to try to clarify it or at
least to ask the member for further clarification. His response
might be prefaced by a phrase such as, "You mean then
. . . ," or even better, it might be put in the form of a question so that the matter can be picked up and carried on,
"Do you mean. . . ?" Again, the leader should be in no
hurry to intrude unless he is sure that the meaning of a statement is escaping the individuals in the group. He should be
careful, also, that his tone or manner does not imply a judgement of what has been said.

Relief of Individual Tension

In the give and take of small-group discussion, various
kinds of tension can be built up: embarrassment, anger resentment, confusion, etc. Although such tensions, when
generalized (distributed among the group) may be healthful stimuli, they can be painful when experienced by the

individual alone. Sometimes, for example, one of the more reticent members of the group may finally goad himself into joining the discussion; he starts out bravely enough and then becomes hesitant, perhaps flounders, unable to find a word for what he wants to say. He is confused and embarrassed. The leader can help by throwing a verbal life line: "What you mean then, Joe . . ." or "Do you want to try that over again, Joe; I think I know what you mean, but I'm not sure."

Discussion of religious questions or of sex may lead to individual or generalized tension. The leader will have to use his own judgement about whether or not to interject himself into the conversation, and at what point and in what manner. Sometimes merely inviting the group's attention to the fact that a discussion may be embarrassing or otherwise painful to certain individuals may lead to a discussion of why, and thus break the ice for the actual topic.

Introduction of Special Devices

A good group leader will be familiar with the use of such special devices as role-playing, buzz sessions, brain storming, and panel presentations. Part of the leader's job is to introduce such devices when appropriate and train the group in their use. (These devices will be taken up in detail elsewhere in this book.)

Use of Silence

A leader's silence can *sometimes* be more helpful to the progress of the group than anything he might say. Occasionally silence from the leader at the very outset of a meeting may help the group to start thinking about its goals or about its immediate tasks and thus help it to take a step toward independence. Silence at various points during the discussion may create a healthful tension that will impel the group to further thought and expression. Silences, especially if prolonged, may be initially painful to the group and to the leader; however, an unembarrassed, acceptant treatment of silence as a time for constructive thought will eventually make the group feel more free and easy itself and, more important, will indicate to the group that responsibility for continuing a discussion rests primarily with it rather than with the leader. In a word, silence at appropriate times is just as much a constructive leadership technique as anything we have mentioned so far.

Listening with Understanding

A group leader should train himself to listen attentively and with understanding to every remark during a discussion period; it should be obvious to everyone that he is eager to catch the total meaning of every statement. He does this not only to help himself know what to do or say next but also to set an example or pattern of good listening habits for the group. The group eventually comes to feel that every individual's contribution is important and worth listening to. In time, it learns to follow the good example set by the leader.

The group-centered leader, however, has to be alert to emotional content as well as intellectual content of a remark or question. Understanding, therefore, requires empathy as well as intellect. Research on this question has led to the following conclusion:

> . . . we may generalize and say that in many democratically oriented groups the leader with empathy toward the members of the group of which he is the leader may be able not

only to influence and help individual members of the group but also to encourage mutually helpful relations among group members and to win support for positive group effort.[2]

Empathy, therefore, not only leads to understanding on the part of leader, but also influences the group. "The general emotional tone of an entire group," says Gordon, "is often influenced by the presence or absence of these qualities (empathy and warmth) in the leader . . . *This would mean that group members may gradually begin to behave toward others in the group in much the same way as the leader behaves toward them.* They would become more warm and friendly to each other, more empathic in their relations with others. Under such conditions communication is undoubtedly facilitated." [3]

Structuring

Structuring, like setting of limits, is a threefold process: Structure can be imposed by agents outside the group, by the group itself, and by the leader. Structure is given to an orientation course by whatever committee or person planned the course, and it will include method of teaching, number of class meetings, topics for discussion, readings, papers and tests, *etc.* Structure imposed by the instructor may include such things as seating arrangement, use of name cards, and whatever bounds he may want to put upon himself and upon the class in order to insure efficient operation of the course. He may wish to make assignments, or he may prefer to have

[2] G. Ross Murray and Charles E. Hendry, *New Understandings of Leadership,* Association Press, New York, 1957, p. 46.

[3] In *Client-Centered Therapy, op. cit.,* p. 348.

the class or a committee of the class make the assignments. Generally speaking, however, the less structure he imposes, the better. Instructors who have experimented with varying degrees of leader-imposed structure report that the less-structured groups tend to be more frustrating to the leader at first, but eventually they achieve a more intense experience through more intellectually and emotionally fruitful meetings.

It goes without saying that a group may impose additional structuring upon itself, and of the three this is the most desirable kind of structure and should be the most satisfactory to the group-centered leader.

SPECIAL DEVICES USED TO FACILITATE GROUP DEVELOPMENT

ORIENTATION through group-centered leadership has multiple goals, both general and specific. As noted previously it is concerned with modifying attitudes in such a way as to help the student become more receptive to what college offers, and it also tries to increase the student's social awareness, self-knowledge, self-confidence, leadership skills, academic skills, and awareness of the place of education in his own life.

Considering these goals, it is not surprising to find that there are many courses of action available for attaining them. In addition to the various procedures previously described that are necessary for effective leading of group discussions, there is a variety of special devices which can be used to facilitate group development.

It should be kept in mind that special group devices such as "buzz" sessions, role-playing, or brainstorming, to name a few, are only supplementary. They may be used to clarify certain issues or questions or as ways of increasing individual participation, interest and involvement, but in themselves they are but auxilliary to the basic interactions through group discussion.

Because of the complex nature of group processes, successful group leadership is partly an art, and like all such skills requires both knowledge and practice. It is seldom that the first attempt to use a new approach will be as successful as the second and third. It is, therefore, highly recommended that an experimental attitude be adopted and that all appropriate techniques be tried more than once. (It will also be extremely helpful if they can be tried out in an in-service training program for orientation leaders.)

Circular Seating Arrangement

It is highly desirable to establish a face to face relationship so that each student can see everyone else. This can be done either by sitting around a table or by arranging the classroom chairs in a circle.

A circular arrangement has several advantages: (a) It tends to de-emphasize the lecturer role of the teacher; (b) it implies that in some sense everyone is on an equal level; (c) it minimizes the possibility of certain students voluntarily withdrawing from the group or ignoring it; (d) it implies that each student who talks is acting and reacting to everyone else in the group; (e) and it implies a responsibility for both listening to and contributing to the group discussions.

It is also suggested (especially in initial sessions) that each student have a card with his first and last name in large letters prominently displayed near his place. These may be collected by the instructor at the end of the session for safe keeping and returned at each new meeting.

It is also suggested that the teacher take a different seat each meeting, again to de-emphasize his authority role.

Use of a Recorder

The use of the services of a recorder, or secretary, to summarize the content of meetings provides continuity between one meeting and the next and a permanent record of the content and direction of the discussions. Further, reading of the notes of a previous meeting at the beginning of the subsequent one can serve as a brief warm-up period, something which frequently seems helpful.

A recorder may be asked to volunteer his services for a particular meeting, or he may be chosen by the following alternative procedure. Let the orientation teacher provide a record notebook and circulate it at random at each meeting so that every student has an opportunity to take notes and subsequently to start a class by reading them. The teacher should collect the notebook at the end of each meeting.

The Use of a Chairman

It is not generally satisfactory to begin using a rotating or fixed chairmanship early in the semester. Most of the students have had little or no experience in conducting a group democratically and are usually unaware of many subtle aspects of group interaction. They learn these things only by watching the orientation teacher in action for a period of time, by serving an apprenticeship, so to speak. Therefore, we suggest that if a student chairmanship system is used, it be begun relatively late in the semester, and that some effort be made to help student chairmen evaluate and improve their skills.

The Use of Small Subgroups

A device developed in recent years which has decided value in orientation is one that is sometimes called the "buzz group." It consists essentially in the division of the total group into a number of smaller subgroups, each designed to deal with some limited question in a more intimate fashion than could be done in the whole group. The typical size of a subgroup is usually 5 or 6, although slightly larger or smaller groups may be used. The "buzz" groups are usually given a fairly specific problem and a limited time, around 5 or 6 minutes, in which to come up with some kind of answer or response.

There are many ways in which buzz sessions can be valuable. At the first meeting, for example, the leader might briefly describe the orientation class as a discussion course concerned with topics of special relevance to freshmen in college. He might then ask the entire group to divide into smaller groups (without necessarily using the term "buzz group") for the purpose of suggesting some topics and issues that they feel they would like to talk about during the semester. He points out that each small group should have only 4 or 5 members, that they should get into a small circle, and that each should have one member take notes on the conclusions reached so that they can be reported to the entire class. A time limit of 5 or 6 minutes is imposed, and a reminder is usually given one minute before the time is up. The subgroups are originally established on a more-or-less random basis by simply asking people who are adjacent to each other to form themselves into small groups. After the time is up the recorder in each subgroup is asked to report to the class, and summary notes are usually made on a blackboard.

This general procedure can be used as often as desired to establish problems or areas for discussion.

Another important use for subgroups or buzz groups is to get various relatively quick answers to a specific question. Thus, the leader might ask: "What is the value of a liberal education?" and then divide the class into buzz groups in an effort to get a tentative answer. The same general procedure would be followed as before in terms of grouping, time, and summary. There might even be times when this subgrouping procedure could be used more than once in a single class meeting.

One other important way in which buzz groups can be useful in orientation is as a method of quickly "feeding back" or summarizing the views of the class on some issue, or group of reports. If, for example, the class has been asked to read a chapter from a text or some other written material, a quick way of getting their feelings about the reading is to have them divide into small groups, discuss their personal reactions for a few minutes and then get a summary report from each buzz group. This enables everyone to express his opinion on a question in a briefer way than would be possible if each person spoke directly to the class.

These three suggestions do not exhaust the possible use of subgrouping; for example, the application to large groups will be suggested in a later chapter.

Why is the use of small subgroups a valuable technique in orientation? For one thing, it helps build up a sense of friendship or commonality—people tend to get to know each other more quickly in smaller groups than in larger ones. Secondly, it is an effective device for focusing attention on some problem and is often productive of surprisingly good ideas in a rather short time. Thirdly, it is a flexible device which can be adapted to many different types of situations as well as to groups of various sizes, including large lecture classes. As the group becomes more cohesive and expressive during the semester, there may be less occasion to use buzz groups, but, all in all, it is a valuable device to know and to use.

Role-Playing

Role-playing is a dramatic technique in which a group of people spontaneously act out a human relations problem and then analyze their enactment with the help of the audience. This method achieves three major objectives: (a) It helps the role-players gain insight and empathy by putting themselves in another's place; (b) It helps them explore and practice various approaches to solving a problem; (c) It imparts as well as interprets information.

Role-playing can be used in connection with almost any controversial issue but is most valuable in connection with human relations questions.

(1) *Getting a problem and establishing a situation.* As far as possible the problem should emerge from group discussion. During the course of an orientation meeting someone might bring up a question about fraternity life, or about attitudes toward parents, or about dating behavior. If answers to these questions are to be sought through role-playing, the students should be encouraged to give specific details about the situations and some discussion should be

started. The leader can then interrupt and say something like, "Sometimes, a problem of the kind Austin has brought up can be understood more readily if we try to understand it from the points of view of all the participants, if we actually try to act and feel as they would in the situation. Psychologists call this 'role-playing.' Let's try it now."

The leader might then ask Austin to come to the front of the room or the center of the circle and to describe the circumstances in which some particular event took place. He tries to conjure up in everyone's mind a vivid impression of the scene and asks the participant to describe the room, the location of the furniture, where he and the other people present were sitting or standing, the time of day and other relevant details. To emphasize the feeling that all this is taking place *right now,* the leader should start to use the present tense. He will not ask, "Where was the furniture?" but rather, "Where are you sitting in the room?" "Where is the desk?" "About what time is it?" *etc.* The emphasis on the nowness of the situation heightens the dramatic impact and facilitates entry into the roles.

(2) *Selecting participants.* Once the stage has been set and everyone is aware of the location of the action, volunteers may be asked for to play any of the roles which have been described. If volunteers are slow in responding, some gentle encouragement of the more talkative members of the group will usually get them to participate. Once the group has seen role-playing in action, there will rarely be any difficulty in getting actors.

(3) *Briefing and acting.* The leader will try to make sure the general roles are understood and that the details of the action are to emerge spontaneously. He might briefly restate

a description of the scene and the nature of the roles, and then let the actors commence. To emphasize spontaneity, the director may have to remind the role-players to keep in their roles. If one of the participants should comment: "If I were in this situation, then I would say . . ." the director should interrupt and tell him to be the person in the role and to act as if the situation is happening right now. Finally, the leader should caution the participants that they are not putting on an act to draw laughs.

(4) *Cutting off the action.* It is important to cut the action when enough of the situation has been presented so that the group can imagine what its conclusion might be and can begin to analyze the problem. This seldom takes more than a few minutes, and a handy rule-of-thumb is to allow the action to run for about 3-10 minutes before cutting. A director should beware of letting the scene go on too long so that there is very little left for the audience to speculate upon and discuss.

Another very useful procedure to encourage insight and understanding is to ask the actors to *reverse roles,* that is, to exchange roles and start from the beginning again. This often produces a new approach to the problem. A variant on this procedure is to cut the action after a few minutes and, without discussion, request two other students to come up and role-play the same situation in another way. This is sometimes called "multiple role-playing."

(5) *Discussion and evaluation.* The role-playing itself should always be thought of as a prelude to discussion and evaluation. The director should ask questions of the following kind (first, addressing himself to the role participants):

"How did you feel about the problem?" or "Why did you react as you did?" (then to the audience) "What would be the likely outcome of the behavior we saw here?" or "What alternative course of action could be tried?" or "Have any of you had to face this kind of problem and if so how did you handle it?" Once discussion is triggered it can be handled like any other group discussion. (It is important to remember that in the course of evaluation a new problem or new approach may be suggested that may profitably be submitted to more role-playing.)

There are several cautions that should be kept in mind in using role-playing. Start with a simple problem if possible. Emphasize spontaneity and the losing of oneself in the role. Let the group do most of the work in carrying through the acting and discussion. Watch out for too much personal involvement; the participants should play their role, such as teacher, student, father, mother, industrialist or union member, and not themselves. And finally, do not use role-playing too often; it is not a panacea, nor a method of entertainment. Used judiciously it can be stimulating and fruitful.

The Use of Cases

The "case method" has begun to find increasing use as an educational tool designed to foster direct "clinical" appraisal of a specific problem as opposed to abstract knowledge of principles. It utilizes real or "imagined" case reports as the basis for detailed discussion. The analysis attempts to answer the question, "What will be the most feasible and beneficial thing that can be done in this given situation and what will be its probable direct and indirect consequences?"

The basic rationale for the method is presented by Professor Berrien in the following terms:

> In the field of human relations any college student has a wealth of unorganized and unthought about experiences which can be utilized as background information. He has already an intuitive acquaintance with the way people act in general. Any generalizations which fail to agree with his experiences will at least be questioned, if not rejected, as a genuine basis for controlling his own relationships, no matter how faithfully and accurately he parrots the teacher-given generalizations on an examination paper. This apparent incongruity between student experience and textbook principles accounts for the failure of much college teaching in making any difference in the way students think or act. For a long while on liberal arts campuses there has been a slogan, "Don't let your studies interfere with your education." Although uttered in jest, the implications of the statement are too often true. Educational materials too often have been remote from student realities and have been presented in such a manner that they sometimes appear to violate common sense. Unless new concepts are presented in such a way as to avoid such a discrepancy, the concepts will remain useful to the student only on examinations, without disturbing his manner of living or thinking.[1]

The cases themselves may be on any subject appropriate to the purpose of orientation and should be given in enough detail (typically one to five pages of print) to enable a fairly complete discussion of the problem raised.

The cases are always incomplete. They are written from

[1] F. K. Berrien, *Comments and Cases in Human Relations*. Harper Brothers, New York, 1951, p. 467.

one person's point of view and not all the information which a reader may wish is always given. It is actually this kind of raw, unclassified, incomplete material with which the average person must deal in making his adjustments and decisions. However, the very sketchy case, devoid of details and background, is to be avoided. Although the incompleteness of information is disturbing to some people, this deficiency may be turned into an asset by asking the group to specify what additional information would be necessary and how it might be obtained.

Handling the Case Method. Once a case has been selected, either by making it up, getting it from a textbook, or, best of all, by getting it directly from the students as a personal or "near-personal" problem, the leader might start with a relatively non-committal comment, such as "What do you think about this case?" or "What aspect of the case do you think we should discuss first?" Once discussion is started all the methods of good group leadership are used: acceptance, summarization, clarification, repetition, and so on.

When class discussion reaches an apparent lull, the leader may ask if there are any other alternatives available, or, if he wishes, may suggest some himself. Before the case discussion is concluded, it is a good idea to ask the group if there are any general principles or ideas that they can draw from the case which will be useful in other contexts.

In general, the instructor should bear in mind that the burden of discussion and evaluation is on the students and that he should not try to impose his own interpretations of the case. Suggesting alternate ways of looking at a case is a perfectly proper function for the discussion leader, but suggesting any one interpretation as *the* answer is not.

This case method, like the others which have been described, can be used from time to time with good effect and heightening of interest, but, like role-playing, should not be overused. Its major value is that it helps develop an understanding of conflicts in realistic rather than abstract terms and encourages the assaying of alternative lines of action and their consequences in specific situations. A typical case is given in the Appendix, the case of Peter Baxter.

Brainstorming

The last few years have seen an increase in the use of a technique called "brainstorming"; this is simply a way of quickly getting a great may ideas from a group of people on some problem. It seems to be a stimulating and enjoyable technique as well as a useful one.

Brainstorming can be used in orientation when a problem comes up which may have many different answers. Suppose, for example, that the question arises of how study habits can be improved. Since each student may have a somewhat different experience in this connection and since many answers are possible, a brainstorming session might be suggested by the leader. He could briefly define the method for the group and then ask them to divide into two smaller groups of, say, seven to ten each. Both groups will work on the same problem. Once the subgroups are formed, the leader explains the four basic rules of procedure which must be adhered to very strictly:

1. No criticisms are allowed during the actual brainstorming. All adverse criticism is reserved for the later evaluation.

2. Quantity is more important at this stage than quality: therefore, anything goes.
3. Each person is to try to build on each other's ideas so that a "chain" reaction is started and the result is truly a group product.
4. Assign one or two people in each group to take note of all the ideas suggested, however wild or impractical.

All this is to be done in a relatively short time, usually between six and twelve minutes. The leader should remind the groups of the time a minute or two before the interval is up, and then at the end ask the recorders to read their lists. This will provide the basis for some fruitful discussion. If desired, the list may be edited by a committee or by the instructor, then mimeographed and given to the students as a permanent and useful record. Other questions for which brainstorming may be used in orientation include: What are the purposes of college? What are the purposes of a liberal arts education? How can prejudice be reduced? What is wrong with fraternities? What substitutes are possible for freshman hazing? How can study habits be improved?

Panel Discussions

In certain circumstances panel discussions can be quite helpful. If an issue arises which requires some specialized factual information which can be obtained only through library reference sources, then a panel of volunteers can be set up. Anywhere from three to six people may obtain information dealing with, for example, occupational classifications and income, fraternity practices, art history, the history of liberal arts colleges, how-to-study techniques, and so forth. The specialized information that the panelists bring to the group should always provide the basis for class discussion.

Utilization of People with Special Skills or Resources

Another facilitating device for group discussion is the utilization of special skills and resources. Students themselves may have special resources or knowledge which they can bring to bear on certain discussions; and certainly the orientation instructor himself may have a great deal of specialized knowledge in at least one broad subject area. If a class discussion turns to this area, it is entirely appropriate for him judiciously to supply some factual information where it seems appropriate. To be a resource person on occasion is one of the roles of the orientation teacher.

Other resource people can be found on any college campus. Among the student body, there are usually upperclassmen who are active in student government and in extracurricular activities and who often make excellent resource people on problems involving such matters. There are also faculty members who will occasionally consent to speak to an orientation class on some topic in which they have special competence. Then, there are usually various college services connected with the Dean of Students Office, such as vocational guidance or co-curricular guidance, which may supply resource people. All in all, the use of such resources can be very fruitful for group development.

Films

Another very useful device to foster group discussion is the occasional use of carefully chosen films.

Our experience suggests that the films to be useful must meet certain criteria: they should relate to one or another of the attitude areas listed earlier; they should present an issue, controversy or problem and not be merely a straightforward factual presentation; they should present problems which have more than one possible solution; they should preferably allow the conflict to remain unanswered, leaving the solution for subsequent discussion; they should be relatively short (5 to 20 minutes as a rough guess) so as to leave plenty of time for discussion. (One group of films which meet these criteria fairly well is the Canadian Film Board's series "What Do You Think?" These and other useful films are listed in the Appendix.)

Readings

Readings are an excellent source of information, ideas, and viewpoints, but because of the nature of the orientation program must be used somewhat differently then in the usual subject matter course. (This matter will be more fully discussed in Chapter Seven.)

Readings should provide the student with motivation for thinking; they should excite, stimulate and even startle him. This can best be done through a confrontation of opposites, through a controversial approach to important questions of life.[2] Such a book may, at the discretion of the instructor, be

[2] See, for example, the present authors' collection, *Controversy,* G. P. Putnam's Sons, New York, 1959.

supplemented by other readings, particularly contemporary magazine and newspaper reports and editorials. In summary, then, readings provide both background and stimulation for significant group discussions.

Evaluations

Because of the many possible patterns of behavior that may emerge in an orientation class, the leaders may sometimes have to deal with unusual friction between members of the group, or horseplay, or withdrawal, or some other difficult situation. One way of dealing with disruptive behavior is to suggest to the group that it take an objective look at itself. This can be done by at least two methods: (1) by asking the students to evaluate on a written questionnaire certain aspects of the group's interactions; or (2) by having one or two members of the group on a particular occasion act as impartial and non-participating observers.

In the first case, one of the students might summarize the results of the class's self-evaluation and report back to the whole group. In the second case, the observers may be asked, near the end of the session, to report their observations and interpretations. In both cases some definite set of questions should be decided on in advance to make the observations and evaluations directed and useful. It is not recommended, however, that evaluation procedures of this sort be used too often. (An example of an evaluation questionnaire is given in Appendix 10.)

STRUCTURE AND PATTERNS
IN THE ORIENTATION GROUP

The Structure of the Orientation Class

SOME critics of an orientation program as described here have raised the question, "Isn't Orientation just a glorified bull session?" This misconception of the orientation class requires clarification: [1]

It should be pointed out that group discussions differ very markedly from a bull session. Bull sessions are primarily concerned with self expression. They usually proceed on a kind of 'one-upmanship' basis in which each person tells a story and each other participant tries to "top" it. Bull sessions are concerned with descriptive material in which the individual talks about what he already knows, what he has seen, what he has read, what he has heard about, etc. Such discussions have as their primary role the enhancement of the speaker. Little listening occurs in a bull session.

A group discussion, on the other hand, has a quite different purpose and operates in a quite different way. The purpose here is not so much to express oneself as to *discover* something. The emphasis is upon the exploration of an idea rather than its statement as a matter of fact. The emphasis

[1] Arthur W. Combs, *The Psychology of the College Student,* The Thorn Lectures, Hofstra College, 1954.

is upon discovery rather than declaration. There is much more listening than talking. Group discussions are more likely to proceed with 'doubtful' talk rather than 'assertive' talk as group members express themselves with such comments as 'I think——,' 'I wonder about——,' 'It seems to me——,' or 'I am not quite sure but——.'

There is another important way in which the orientation course differs from a bull session, and that is its structure. This structure consists of limits, expectations, and content.

1. *Limits.* Orientation has limits, just as does any other class in the college. What the limits are, however, will vary somewhat with the particular institution as well as state regulations. At one college, for example, the limits are as follows:

—The course is required of all entering freshmen.

—It receives two semester hour credits for one semester of work.

—There are three hours of meetings a week, divided either into three one-hour classes or two one-and-one half hour classes.

—There is a letter grade given to each student at the end of the semester which becomes part of his freshman and college academic record.

—Attendance and lateness regulations are the same as in any other class.

—General college rules, such as no smoking in the classroom, etc., are to be respected.

2. *Expectations.* Although the class limits are relatively easy to specify and follow, the various expectations which are incorporated into the orientation class are somewhat

more general and consequently permit greater variation in application. The following list of expectations is largely in the nature of recommendations to the teacher, and is, therefore, subject to modification as experience may dictate:

—It is highly recommended that a circular seating arrangement be used so that everyone is face to face.

—It is suggested that name cards be used with the first (or nickname) and last name of each student included.

—It is recommended that a secretary or recorder be used who will take notes on the content of each class meeting.

—There may be some optional use of a student assistant. These are usually upperclassmen who attend meetings and are often invaluable as resource people on topics like Campus Government, Student Organizations etc.

—At the end of the semester each teacher is expected to write a short qualitative report on each of his counselees (see Appendix 8) which covers such areas as general adjustment, realization of potential, prediction of academic success, extenuating circumstances, significant personality characteristics, and areas indicating need for future guidance.

—It is expected that each student be treated as though what he has to say is important enough to deserve serious consideration. Ridicule and embarrassment are to be avoided. Students can be challenged without being threatened.

—It is expected that the teacher will act as a resource person as well as an initiator of new ideas and techniques designed to facilitate group interaction.

3. *Content*. It has been suggested that one of the primary reasons for such large withdrawals of students from college

(as much as 50 percent) is that students are not convinced that the subject matter offered for study is relevant to or valuable for finding an effective place in the world outside. Dr. Combs notes that much of our difficulty in traditional education stems from the fact that some instructors see their jobs mainly as one of supplying information, often without regard to the *student's perception* of the relevance of such information.

What this implies, we believe, is that the instructor of the orientation class should be primarily a resource person and guide, rather than an information-giver *per se.* He must try to rely as far as possible on information the group can provide, but he must not feel limited to this information. He can supplement this pool of information from his own knowledge; he can recommend sources of further information: resource people and the use of media such as newspapers and magazines. It is also important to remember that many of the issues discussed are questions of values—moral issues, if you will—which do not generally have unequivocal answers. Sometime the very act of noting an alternative viewpoint or showing that an issue cannot be meaningfully judged in black-or-white terms does more service than supplying factual information.

We can, however, establish the content of the course in such a way as to facilitate attainment of the basic aim of orientation, which is to help the student become more receptive to what is offered by a college education. The subject matter of the course deals with the problems that students face as college students. Some of these problems are broad and complex, like problems of human relations; others are more limited and specific, like study techniques and the use of the library. The students may be given a list of topics for possible discussion but are informed that the group is not limited to these alone, nor bound by any specific sequence. The orientation teacher must be sensitive not only to the expressed needs and opinions of the students but to many of the broad problems of our society. (More specific discussion of the content of orientation will be given in the next chapter.)

With this general structure in mind, let us discuss the initial contact with an orientation class and describe some "typical" meetings.

The First Day

Because the first day of an orientation class can set the tone for the entire semester, special attention should be paid to this meeting. We begin here with individuals whose only relationship with one another is that of physical proximity. The instructor's first aim, therefore, is to create an environment in which each individual can comfortably become a member of a group.

It is possible to move quickly from the typical seating arrangements to a circular one. With a brief explanation, both this and the use of name cards become easily accepted. It is rarely necessary to give more than a brief explanation of the general aims of the class as a discussion group before entering into the small-group discussion climate described in an earlier chapter.

The following actual transcript of the notes of a first meeting suggests how rapidly the group can become involved in issues and how thought-provoking some of the ideas can be.

This was the first meeting of the Orientation class and Dr. L_____ explained that this is a discussion group in which everyone would participate and talk about topics of mutual interest.

When the question was posed, several members of the class pointed out that some of the values of a discussion group of this kind are:

1. We can all express our views.
2. We can discuss or raise problems and try to solve them.
3. We can learn to talk more easily in front of people.
4. We can learn more about ourselves.

At this point we got into smaller groups and suggested topics of interest to us for possible discussion. These were:

1. How to join fraternities or sororities.
2. What college will offer us.
   What we will offer other people when we graduate.
3. Parental influences.
4. When and how does the Freshman class get organized?
5. Problems of adjustment to college.
6. How to get an increase in school spirit.
7. How do we feel about hazing?

We spent the rest of the time talking mostly about hazing and school spirit. It was pointed out that school spirit depends on good leadership, and on competition or challenge, and also on a desire to belong to a group.

Sometimes a group can be unified by mutual hate of some outside agency. Hazing, it was suggested, could be a kind of challenge, and if we meet it successfully, we feel pride. Hate is a temporary result of a difficult challenge.

On the other hand, it was suggested that hazing might just be a form of revenge and that it was really a waste of time and an unnecessary annoyance, particularly during the first two weeks of the semester. However, more people seemed to be in favor of hazing than against it.

It might be noted that the use of small sub-groups ("buzz groups") was introduced early in the first meeting with good effect. But each instructor should experiment with various procedures to discover the methods that are most congenial to him. Once a suitable framework has been established, including the ideas of acceptance and permissiveness, the potentials within the group usually emerge quickly.

Trends in Emotional Climate

Just as individuals differ in personality traits and dominant emotions, so, too, do groups. Since a group is a collection of individuals sharing certain goals and operating within prescribed limits, the predominant emotions of the individuals will be reflected in the emotional tone of the group.

At the start of the orientation class, the students are faced with an unusual, an almost unique, experience. They find themselves in a permissive school room atmosphere in which they will be allowed to set up some goals of their own and discuss questions that spontaneously develop. Many react to this situation with bewilderment or surprise. These emotions may be followed by: (a) a submissive dependence on the teacher, or (b) some form of hostility directed either toward the instructor, the college, or other class members, or (c) apprehension and concern as to what will happen next.

As the permissive atmosphere is consistently maintained, new feelings begin to appear. The individuals start to express more personal feelings as they get to know the other students and as they come to feel more trust in the teacher. A friendly, enthusiastic attitude develops. The individual begins to lose his feelings of aloneness and his belief in the uniqueness of his own problems.

If the discussions are skillfully handled the students begin to get new perspectives, to see new ways of looking at old problems. Their decision making ability is gradually strengthened, and the group, in turn, becomes more cohesive.

It should be remembered that the group's pattern of emotional development does not always move at the same rate or without fluctuations. Right after the midterm grades are in, there is usually more apprehension than at other times, and there is often a tendency for group cohesion to be noticeably less after a long vacation period such as the Christmas recess.

It should also be noted that although orientation groups are randomly selected, one group may differ from another quite markedly. Some groups are quiet and lukewarm about everything; others are aggressive and excited. Some may be mentally unalert; others, highly intellectual. Such differences may be individual differences between groups and consequently have little or nothing to do with the teacher or his methods.

Not only may the emotional climate of the group differ from session to session and over the course of the semester, it may vary even during the course of a single session. At the beginning of every meeting there is usually a quiet period of from a few seconds to a few minutes in which there is relatively little group participation. It is almost as if the students need a little time to shed the role they are used to playing in the usual lecture class and to "recast" themselves in their new roles, as members of an orientation class. The reading of announcements and reports from the recorder about the previous meeting will often shorten this "warm up period" and facilitate subsequent group interaction and discussion. Sometimes, buzz groups can also be used for this purpose.

These trends in mood and reactivity are sometimes labeled the "emotional climate" of the group. Yet it is important to recognize that this group climate is the resultant of various individual reactions, which need to be recognized and understood.

Individual Roles in the Group

A good group leader will in time come to recognize certain types of students who tend to facilitate or impede group development. Without pretending that one may describe a total personality in a single phrase, it is still helpful to recognize that many individuals in a group tend to adopt a certain more-or-less stereotyped way of reacting which can be briefly characterized.

On the one hand, there are those whose modes of behavior are largely helpful to the group. This group includes those who tend to be *initiators* of new ideas and problems solving suggestions; *clarifiers* of issues which have become obscured; *information seekers* who will gather factual data; *summarizers* of the progress of the discussion; *harmonizers* who try to mediate differences between other members; *encouragers* who are very free with praise and personal warmth; and *compromisers* who try to deal with differences of opinion by always seeking the middle ground.

On the other hand, there are roles, or ways of acting in the group, which are largely disruptive. The *blocker* tends to disagree to an unreasonable extent on many issues and often tries to maintain interest in or return to an issue after the rest of the group has apparently finished with it; the *aggressor* makes a point of disapproving of other peoples' values or acts and often attacks the group or the teacher or the problems being discussed; the *dominator* tries to control the group and direct it toward interests of his own by excessive talking, interrupting, and by trying to get people on "his side"; the *playboy* usually tries to achieve attention by cynical or comic remarks, horseplay, loud talking to his neighbor, or by engaging in irrelevant behavior such as reading the newspaper or doing homework; and the *isolate,* because of fear or indifference, tries physically and/or emotionally to separate himself from the group by silence.

These different roles represent simplifications and obviously may overlap. They may also be modified and replaced. In fact, one of the signs of group development is an increase in the number of students who adopt helpful, group maintenance roles, and show an increasing role flexibility. The ability to shift roles and behave in a number of different constructive ways, depending on the state of the group and the issues under discussion, is a sign of increasing maturity.

There is usually some concern on the part of the teacher on how to handle the negative-role players in the group. A few suggestions will be given here and a number of general procedures later.

It should be remembered first of all that in many cases, strong negative attitudes within the group (if they are not general) probably reflect particular personality traits or needs of the individual student. He may, for example, be trying to gain attention, or feel superior, or avoid looking foolish, or avoid feeling controlled or dominated by the teacher or other students. If the teacher avoids a tendency to respond in kind and instead accepts the student's remarks at face value and takes them very seriously, reflecting and "deflecting" the negative attitudes, in many cases a change occurs in the student. If a student discovers that his underlying fears are not justified, he will often modify his behavior.

A second way of dealing with the negative roles is to suggest some group evaluations, either through the use of questionnaires (see Appendix 10) or of an observer. The use of an impartial observer often gives the group member a clearer perspective on his own behavior.

A third and probably more drastic way of dealing with certain negative roles is to role-play a segment of the group discussion, with other students taking the roles of playboy, aggressor, and so forth. This becomes a kind of "mirror" technique and can be productive of insight and improvement of attitudes.

Finally, negative roles may be handled through the individual counseling which each student should have with the teacher. An individual's behavior in the group may be brought up in the privacy of the counselor's office and tactfully discussed. Sometime the student may be willing to express underlying attitudes here and not in the group.

Besides *individual* roles that may produce problems, there are, also, common types of blocks or breakdowns in *group* development.

Some Group Problems

Interminable Discussion. The group discussion drifts from topic to topic, specific problem areas are avoided, and no decisions of any kind are reached.

This kind of behavior may indicate confusion or it may reflect an aversion to becoming too deeply involved in a controversial area. In order to rationalize avoidance of an issue, a student may (a) discover that there are all sorts of "dangers" in any specific formulation of conclusions: danger of exceeding authority, of misinterpretation, of misuse, or of criticism; (b) may retreat from the problem by endless discussion of various techniques for approaching it; (c) may suggest that it would be better to wait until some expert can be consulted. Or his rationalization may take any number of other forms.

Since such subterfuges are really an expression of fear or insecurity, one way of handling them is for the leader to reflect verbally the feeling that he thinks underlies such a statement, and thus bring the feeling out into the open for frank examination. Sharper definition of the meaning of rambling discussion can be achieved, also, through the use of role playing, calling on the group recorder or critic, or staging a buzz session. Still another practical way of meeting the problem of rambling discussion is explained under the topic "Integration" (pp. 45-46) in the section devoted to Specific Leadership Techniques.

Pairing (or Side Talking). This kind of behavior may reflect a lack of interest in the topic under discussion, a feeling of insecurity on the part of the individuals involved, or a need that is not being met by the group. One is reminded of a little child tugging for attention on the coat sleeve of an adult. The same need for attention is being expressed by the person who turns to his neighbor instead of expressing himself to the group as a whole. This situation is often best handled by disregarding it in the hope that other members of the group will become aware of it and take steps to correct it. If this does not happen, then the leader might pose pairing as a group problem and employ whatever devices (role-playing, buzz-session, and so on) he believes will best tend toward modification of the situation.

Excessive Voting. There should be little need for voting in an orientation group. The discussion is not usually of the decision-making variety, and when it is, it is better to strive for consensus rather than for imposition of the majority will. When individuals persist in calling for a vote, their behavior may indicate something as simple as impatience with the lack of progress or something as deep-lying as a need for support from the rest of the group. Excessive voting can cut off discussion before the problem has been thoroughly explored, can give the group a false sense of achievement, and can close off the learning process. Talking a problem through to a consensus is more apt to be profitable in terms of understanding and learning.

Excessive Silences. Silence on the part of the group, as pointed out earlier, need not necessarily be considered as blocking behavior and may, in fact, be used for constructive purposes. But if it is obviously a reflection of apathy on the part of the group, then, of course, it is an impediment to progress, and the leader must give the group a shot in the arm. Such things as a quick summary of progress, a buzz session to decide on where to go from here, a challenging question, or simply a statement reflecting in words the feeling of the group may provide the stimulus the group needs to get going.

Particular Individual Roles. There will be students in the group who, because of their personal needs—their insecurity or immaturity—will act as "blocker," "dominator," "playboy," or "isolate." Although the leader may recognize and resent the actions of such individuals, he must be careful not to judge them nor criticize them overtly. Acceptance of their individuality and of their needs as individuals is the biggest step toward changing their behavior. The group itself can be trusted to influence such individuals more practically than can the teacher. The ideal is to help each person gradually to achieve the role of leader, i.e., initiating and clarifying ideas, encouraging others, conciliating disputes, and participating constructively in group discussion.

General Remedies

There is not always a single or simple way of handling all these problems. The types of leader behavior that will be helpful may be grouped in the following ways:

Create a Democratic Atmosphere. The group should feel that the teacher is not there as an authoritarian person to tell them what to do, but is available as a resource person to whom the group can appeal for information that it needs. Following the leadership principles described earlier (pp. 28-42) will contribute to this ideal.

Encourage Goal Setting by the Group. This develops group spirit and individual closeness. The use of "buzz" groups here is especially recommended.

Use Evaluation Techniques. An occasional questionnaire

about group feelings and progress is very useful, as well as the use of a *process observer,* selected from the group. Sometimes a discussion of individual roles is helpful.

Be a "Reflector" and "Deflector". This means occasionally interpreting and clarifying the content of the group discussion, particularly the *feeling tone* back of a question or issue, as well as deflecting certain questions away from particular individuals to the group as a whole. This may involve calling the attention of the group to certain events going on and asking for reactions.

Use Role Playing. This will increase participation and interest and may sometimes be skillfully used to demonstrate certain roles present in the group.

Use the Individual Conferences. In personal talks with an individual you can sometimes point out certain aspects of his behavior, as you see it, and explore with him possible reasons for it.

If these problems that occasionally arise can be satisfactorily dealt with then both the teacher and the group will be rewarded by an increase in cohesiveness, in depth of discussion, in independence and in personal growth—goals which are well worth the efforts.

THE PLACE OF CONTENT
IN THE ORIENTATION COURSE

THE mistake can be made, in fact has been made, in academic as well as in more informal settings, of considering the group-centered process as an end in itself. It is undoubtedly true that democratic interaction among individuals gathered in small groups does have a beneficial effect and can achieve certain educational ends. It would be difficult to maintain, however, that discussion and interaction alone can accomplish the usual educational ends implied in most college courses.

Freshman Orientation as a course has generally fallen short of its goals when taught by other than group-centered methods. But it is not enough merely to introduce the group-centered method into the program and expect the method alone to carry the course. Groups in which this has been tried—by the authors—luxuriate in the freedom allowed by the course and are very appreciative of the warmth and friendliness that spring up among the members. Still, such a group feels that something is lacking; and when the course is ended, its members are left with the impression that they have been "operating in a vacuum," that they have not accomplished very much.

An appropriate subject matter is essential to full achievement of the aims of the course. Students and teachers must have the satisfaction that comes from reading and the completion of assignments, and they need the sense of accomplishment that comes from successfully passing examinations and fulfilling other course requirements.

"How to" Content

One typical course content in orientation classes is the "How to" content: how to get the most out of college, how to study, how to take examinations, and so forth. Such courses may be said to tackle the problems of freshman orientation head-on, by lecture, discussion, and reading, and are based on the premise that telling a student what to do and how to do it is the best contribution the course can make toward his adaptation to college.

This kind of course is usually accompanied by a text that also features a direct attack on problems of skills, habits—even personality characteristics and attitudes—and tells students, usually in an informal and sometimes in an engaging manner, how to change themselves so that they can better profit from the college environment. Our experience with this kind of course and this kind of text has been disappointing. Not only do they fail to get through to the student but even seem to intensify his normal resistance to change. It seems almost impossible to avoid the "talking down" process when one works with the "how to" content. Students are more likely to resist and resent such an approach than to profit from it.

The General Readings Approach to Content

A second typical approach to orientation subject-matter is the "life in our times" approach, the scope of which includes any and all of the social sciences, the humanities, the natural sciences, and whatever processes and procedures one may encounter in life, education, and the pursuit of happiness. This is not a "Contemporary Civilization" type of course; its reading material and topical content are considerably more varied. Reading a good text prepared for this approach with understanding and discussing the many problems it raises may be in itself a liberal education.

But the fault with such an approach to orientation is that it attempts too much. It too easily loses the focus that orientation should have, and in one course seems to be attempting to do the total educational job. The net result is that another course has been added to the freshman curriculum, and perhaps a good one; but the experience the student gets from such a course, valuable though it may be, is not the specific orientation-to-college experience that we have been advocating here.

The Receptivity Approach

The receptivity approach to orientation subject matter is the one our experience leads us to believe is the best. Here, the content has two main components: a list of discussion topics, and a book of readings germane to the task that orientation is tackling. It is understood, however, that additional reading will be assigned if it becomes appropriate during the semester and that students will be free to bring up other topics that represent problems in their college experience.

The guiding principle both in the selection of readings and in the selection of topics for discussion is that they should have a clear bearing on the problem of orientation to college, i.e., they should represent an assault on the problem of the student's receptivity to part or all of the college experience.

The purpose of orientation is to increase the student's receptivity to the total college experience; to do this we ask the student to examine, through discussion and reading, certain misunderstandings, weaknesses, feelings, or attitudes he may have toward various aspects of the college experience. The topics of discussion, therefore, will encompass those "aspects of the college experience," a lack of receptivity to which may deprive the student of some of the benefits of college.

Topics seem to group themselves under three main headings: the functional aspects of college, the human relations problems, and the student's personal world.

Under the functional aspects of college, discussion of the purpose of college would be appropriate, and so we would have a topic such as *What Should College Do for the Individual?* Clarification is often necessary of the place of the humanities or of the social sciences in education: Why does one have to take a language? What good does it do to take a whole year of history? In a word, there is likely to be little understanding of the "liberalizing" nature of certain courses; and so we have the topic *What Is Meant by a Liberal Education?* The educational goals of college are realized not only through the academic experience but also through a more or less formalized "extra-curriculum." And so we have the topic *The Nature and Function of Co-curricular Activities.* Finally, under the general heading of functional problems, we attack inadequacies in the use of the tools and techniques of learning under the heading *Academic Skills and Tech-*

niques, which includes instruction on how to develop study skills, on the use of the library, taking examinations, and taking notes.

Among the most immediately relevant human relations problems are those that occur between student and teacher and so we have the topic *Student-Teacher Relationships.* In addition, and even if a student is living away from home, there is, of course, a strong bond between parent and child. Hence it becomes appropriate to discuss *Student-Parent Relationships* and the very real and often disturbing struggle toward independence that most students are experiencing. Also, many problems of interpersonal relationships center around student attitudes and feelings toward persons of other creeds, colors, or cultures; hence the topic *Prejudice* is germane to an orientation course.

There are obviously further topic breakdowns that can be made in the human-relations area: student-counselor relations, student-administration relations, peer group relations, relations between the sexes, and so forth. (So far as sex relations is concerned, however, our own experience has been that is preferable to include it under a later topic, Morality.) To cover such topics, we have found it profitable to begin with the general rather than the specific and have therefore introduced the topics *The Democratic Process in Human Relations* and *Authoritarianism in Human Relations.* (An additional one or two specific topics may, of course, be substituted for the general approach.)

Those topics which seem to center more strictly within the student's personal world have to do with such things as the codes he lives by, his goals and ambitions, his fears, his attitudes toward the world in which he lives. His attitudes toward cheating, drinking, sex, gambling, and so forth may be sounded through discussion of the topic *Morality*. His views on manners, dress, speech may be expressed through discussion of *Social Competence*. His ideas on what he expects to get out of life and give to life may be clarified by discussion of *Personal Goals*. So that an opportunity may be given him to express whatever misgivings he may have about the uncertain future of our world, some topic such as *Today's World* may be introduced.

We would like to emphasize again that our particular topic breakdown and our specific topic titles are arbitrary. However, there is one criterion we would insist upon: that is, that the topics stand up under the "receptivity test": Do student-teacher relationships have a bearing on his receptivity to college? Will a clarification of his personal goals increase a student's receptivity to the college experience? Will a misunderstanding of what college is for keep the student from getting all he should from his four years as an undergraduate? If a topic cannot clearly pass this test, its appropriateness as orientation subject-matter should be seriously questioned.

Readings for Receptivity

In choosing reading materials to accompany orientation we must again keep always in mind that the purpose of orientation is to increase the student's receptivity to the college experience. In accordance with this "receptivity test," we should like to present the following few suggestions as aids to choosing appropriate reading material:

1. The readings should be supplementary to the discussions, not topics of discussion in themselves. The

focus must always remain on the members of the group and *their* problems, and not be allowed to shift to real or hypothetical problems of others.

2. For the most part, readings should be selected for their catalytic qualities rather than for information. They should be challenging, discussion-producing, perhaps controversial. To paraphrase an old educational precept: in orientation it is more important to be suggestive than to be correct. Balance between points of view is not a prerequisite: discussion should serve to restore balance. In fact, imbalance may encourage the student to do additional reading.

3. Always, of course, readings should be chosen for their relation to the topics that are discussed in the course. They are used in a supplementary fashion and should be stimulating, but they must also have a direct bearing on the discussion topics.

4. For the most part avoid hortatory, preachy, "teachy," or "down-talking" readings.

5. Collections of readings should not be too bulky. A too bulky book can be a deterrent to receptivity in that it tends to discourage students from trying to exhaust its possibilities and leaves the impression of being tedious rather than stimulating.

To the authors' knowledge very few collections of readings have been specifically designed to serve orientation courses, and those that have been devised for orientation, do not, for the most part, take into consideration the circumscribed, limited nature of the orientation goals. Too often, although they may make excellent reading for a course that is designed to cover the waterfront of human knowledge, as supplementary material to topics germane to orientation they are simply overpowering. Like readings for certain broad, social-science-survey courses, they tend to become ends in themselves, topics for discussion rather than catalysts to discussion.

In addition to the readings it would be well to select (and this is an exception to the general rules above) a good how-to-study manual, of which there are many on the market. A simple inexpensive one is Staton, Thomas F., "How To Study", McQuiddy Printing Co., Nashville, Tenn., 1954. A more elaborate and more expensive one is Morgan, Clifford T., and Deese, James, "How To Study", McGraw-Hill Book Co., New York, 1957.

Additional Topics

A final word should be said here about the leeway classes should be given to bring up for discussion topics other than those chosen in advance for the course.

Freshman students often find the group-centered process as used in orientation a rather heady experience. They may over-react to: (1) the freedom with which they can speak their minds (2) the warmth of the relationship between student and instructor, and (3) the freedom they have to initiate discussion of topics that may or may not be in the course plan. Their exhilaration may lead to suggestions that go beyond the bounds of the course or beyond the limits set by the instructor.

Although no one wishes to discourage such feelings of freedom and warmth, which should be a natural development of the group-centered process and of the orientation course itself, at the same time the effect of this exhilaration, especially early in the course, may be such that the class will tend to get out of bounds. Again an awareness by the leader that one of his functions is to call attention to limits will be of service. Freedom to speak one's mind is limited, for example, by consideration of the feelings of others, a constriction of which the group may sometimes have to be reminded. The warmth of relationship between instructor and student may be very satisfying, but its expression must be limited by certain rules of decorum, by academic tradition, the instructor's personal code of behavior, and so forth. (The authors have more than once taught orientation classes that at some point during the semester have suggested the class hold one or more of its meetings in a near-campus tavern. When such a suggestion has been made we have had no difficulty in letting the class know that it had struck against one of the limits. So far as we know, our refusal has had no ill effects—and no second invitations were forthcoming.)

Classes are to be encouraged to bring up topics that do not appear in the course plan, but it must be understood that the topics will be appropriate to the general purpose of orientation. If a topic is brought up that is not appropriate, it is the leader's job to bring the topical limits to the attention of the class.

For example, at the beginning of a particular class, while the instructor waits hopefully for the class to shoulder the responsibility of getting the discussion started, Edith might finally say, "Well, what are we going to talk about today?"

After another short silence, Jack says, "Well, if nobody can think of anything better, I suggest we talk about jazz."

"Good idea," says Bernie. "That's my favorite subject."

The instructor can be direct or indirect. Let's say he tries the latter approach. "Before we go on with the discussion, perhaps we ought to consider in what way a discussion about jazz fits into the general scheme of an orientation course."

This will bring the existence of discussion limits to the attention of the class and at the same time may lead them to some consideration of and discussion about the general scheme or purpose of orientation.

The instructor may wish to test the appropriateness of a particular topic by applying the receptivity-to-college test. Will a discussion of jazz, for example, help the student become more receptive to his total college experience? There are some fine lines to be drawn. Obviously a discussion of jazz as a *tangential* subject, following from or supplementing a discussion of peer-group conformity, for example, might be perfectly appropriate. It would be hard to justify, however, a discussion of jazz *per se* within the framework of orientation goals.

In bringing the attention of the class to topical limits, the instructor may at times have to be direct and arbitrary. However, the indirect approach, as illustrated above, may often be preferable. The leader, should not, however, be too hasty in calling a topic out of bounds, since a tangential discussion of an apparently foreign topic may often lead into a fruitful discussion of an appropriate one.

Tests and Grades

Finally, something should be said about creative and evaluative devices such as papers, projects, and examinations.

Students usually feel that requiring a heavy amount of

outside work in the orientation course is inconsistent with the purposes of the course, and we tend to agree with them. They realize before long that orientation is intended to help them through college, and heavy assignments that take away much of their time from other courses are considered roadblocks rather than helps.

There is some value, however, if only a sense of accomplishment, in passing a test or in turning in a paper or in completing a project to be presented to the class. If final grades are given, such things may help in determining a student's grade for the course. There is nothing in the basic philosophy of an orientation course that proscribes the use of such devices.

There can be a conventional final examination or a take-home examination. The only caution to observe is that it should not test the readings directly but should test the student's ability to use the readings to back his own statements.

Papers can be prepared and presented to the class or to the instructor on any of the discussion topics.

Individual investigation of certain problems (a survey, for example, of what faculty members think of fraternities) may be made and reports given to the class. Or, instead, committees or panels may work on such investigations.

Another useful device that some students enjoy is the keeping of a diary, a day-by-day account of the individual's reactions to the class, his thoughts and opinions on the topics discussed, or his own thoughtful extension of any discussion that has occurred.

A final grade in orientation seems to have some value, although the authors recommend a Pass or Fail rather than the conventional A, B, C, D, or F. Rightly or wrongly, grades seem to furnish a kind of motivation. Secondly, so accustomed have students grown to being rewarded or punished, they feel that something important is missing unless a grade is awarded at the end of the course. Finally, giving a grade inevitably engenders an important topic of discussion, a discussion which quite often leads to considerable insight about grades in general.

If an instructor is group-centered enough to permit the class to have a share in deciding the criteria for grades and for administering them, the experience can be very meaningful to the individual members of the class. A discussion fairly early in the course of what the criteria for grades ought to be will often be valuable in setting the tone and structure of future class meetings.

| Chapter | A TRAINING PROGRAM |
| 8. | FOR ORIENTATION FACULTY |

SINCE most college teachers may not be overly familiar with the group-centered process, nor, for that matter, with freshman orientation as a course, it is advisable and profitable that there be a continuing opportunity for learning something about the method and the philosophy.

The Need for Training

Group-centered teaching or leadership can be learned and, in fact, must be learned if the approach is to be used successfully. A certain amount of leadership techniques can be absorbed by experience as a member of a group-centered class, but too few college teachers have had experience as students in such classes. Even those fortunate enough to have such experience will need to supplement it by additional study in the method and by actual experience as a leader.

The old maxim "Leaders are born, not made," is coming more into question as time goes on. Leadership training programs, workshops in group development, human relations institutes are multiplying all over the country and are pretty good evidence that industry, politics, and education have become aware of the fact that leaders can be made (See Appendix 5).

Nor are we at all convinced that merely adopting the

"democratic" philosophy of the group-centered process is enough by itself to make one a good democratic or group-centered leader. It is true that certain attitudes toward individuals and groups are desirable, perhaps indispensable, for best results; but faith in the individual and in the group, acceptance, warmth, and permissiveness will not in themselves bring out the potential that lies in a group nor make a group the ideal place for the individual to realize his potential. Something more is needed, and that something more is a knowledge of the skills of group-centered leadership.

A training program is also helpful in dispelling certain misconceptions that tend to spring up in regard to the group-centered process and orientation itself. It is very easy for instructors to form an impression of the group-centered method as a laissez-faire process rather than as a process controlled by limits, the leader, and the group. We have known some teachers to get the notion somehow that they are not supposed to lead at all but to appoint some member of the group to do the leading. We have known some teachers to form the impression that any subject whatsoever is fair game for orientation, that any site the group chooses is an acceptable meeting place, that any violation of college rules is permissible.

These notions get accepted somehow and are sometimes put into practice, leaving orientation open to justifiable criticism. One of the explicit tasks of a training program is to dispel such notions.

Aims and Outcomes of Training

One of the aims of a training program is to give the teacher actual experience in the process and devices of group-centered leadership. The program should not consist merely of talk about philosophy, principles, and practices; it should actually give the trainee a taste of what he will face in his orientation classroom.

Secondly, a training program should by lecture, discussion, descriptive reading, and any other available devices give the instructors an understanding of orientation as a course—its aims, its philosophy, its history, its prevalence on today's college campus. Because of its recency as a course in American colleges, such explication is necessary.

Third, a training program should give not only the necessary training and experience in the group-centered method but should also give some understanding of the *philosophy* of the process. Discussion should concern general principles and seek to impart an insight into the aims and philosophical foundations of the group-centered approach.

Fourth, the training program should aim at fostering a receptive attitude among faculty members toward the group-centered process as a general teaching method rather than as a method to be used only for orientation. Our experience has been that a great many faculty members, consciously or unconsciously, adopt the principles and devices of the group-centered method in their regular classes. Thus faculty orientation training and experience may have a more widespread influence than is usually imagined.

Finally, the training program should include instruction and practice in individual counseling. Since most orientation programs include personal counseling by the instructor, he should be given some notion of techniques and points of view, and some instruction about possible need for referral to specialists and the best way to go about such referral.

General Framework for a Training Program

In working out a training program it is usually profitable to enlist the aid of a committee of the faculty. The members of the committee should be favorable to orientation, people who are or who will be actively engaged in the orientation program and who know something about the group-centered process or who wish to learn about it. Although it may seem desirable to the administrator of the program to keep the same committee membership year after year, since a member's value increases with his experience, it may be well to rotate membership to some extent, in order to involve the interest of and give experience to as many persons as possible.

A general framework for training which has proved valuable over a period of years consists of (1) a workshop or series of workshops, (2) a series of discussion meetings, and (3) a "colleague" system among the orientation teachers.

Workshop. In our experience, a two-day workshop, held just before the fall semester begins, when most of the faculty have returned to their homes after vacation and are available, has met with considerable approval. Our workshop has been held on campus since there is no other place available, although we consider it preferable to have it off campus in some type of "retreat," with the participants available during the evening hours as well as the day. As it was, our workshop hours were from nine until three each day, with an hour off for lunch (charged to the orientation budget).

We would recommend a second workshop during the first semester and a third one during the second semester; however, we believe these further workshops are advisable only if they can be made palatable to the faculty by being held in some attractive off-campus spot, where recreation is available and relaxation possible, and with the total expense being borne by the college.

Discussion meetings. We have found it helpful to conduct regularly scheduled discussion meetings during the semester for orientation faculty. The purpose of the meetings is primarily to give the instructors an opportunity to share their experiences, express their feelings, and, in general, to receive advice, information, and comfort from one another. Secondarily, the meetings may serve as opportunities to discuss specific problems of the group-centered process or of individual counseling. Group-centered techniques, of course, should be used in conducting the meetings.

Colleague system. We recommend, once the orientation program has been in operation for a year or two, that the experienced teachers help orient and advise the new teachers by means of some sort of "colleague" system. For example, three of the new instructors may be assigned to one of the experienced teachers, and the four can get together periodically for informal conversations about the course, have lunch together occasionally, or simply make a practice of talking about orientation when they happen to meet.

Content of Workshops

Films are a possibility in the conduct of workshops if appropriate ones are available. We ourselves have used only one film: "How to Conduct a Discussion." [1] This is an Ency-

---

[1] The film may be rented or purchased from Encyclopaedia Britannica Films, Inc., 202 East 44 Street, New York 17, N. Y.

clopaedia Britannica production, a lucid, unpretentious and pleasing exposition of general principles. It makes an excellent kickoff for discussion about discussion, and even if there is no time available for discussion, the film is informative and unambiguous enough to stand alone.

Occasional brief lectures are almost mandatory. They are necessary to clarify the purposes of orientation, to clear up misconceptions, to evaluate and criticize the program, to announce new developments, and to re-emphasize important points. When special devices like role-playing are introduced for the first time, a brief descriptive or explanatory lecture is usually necessary. We feel that the lecture should be used sparingly (in the two-day workshop outlined in the Appendix it will be noted that relatively little time was used for lecture), but it is nonetheless a valuable device.

Reading material should be supplied for the workshops and also during the year. There are a number of good books on group-centered leadership, articles on freshman orientation and books that include discussions of the topic, and any number of articles on special devices such as role-playing, and so on. A list of appropriate reading materials is included in the Appendix of this book.

At the workshops, provision should be made for straight discussion, preferably in small groups, of problems or topics that are germane to the orientation program. For example, faculty members generally seem to be interested in a discussion of the purpose of orientation, and considerable illumination can come from a thoughtful examination of this subject. We have learned to accept without much inquiry the purpose of courses such as freshman English and history, but orientation as a course is so new as to require periodic scrutiny, especially by those who are engaged in teaching it. These discussion groups should be handled by a competent leader, so that the faculty can get the feel of good leadership. Fruitful, too, are discussion of specific problems that are likely to concern group-leaders, problems such as what to do when a student starts complaining about one of his teachers, or how to handle discussions of sex or religion.

Besides straight discussion moderated by a trained leader, a workshop should include some practice discussions and some acting out of probable situations in which various members of the faculty can be given a chance to practice group-centered leadership. For straight discussion, topics should be chosen mainly for their likelihood to excite the participants: "What is wrong with college teaching?" "What is meant by academic freedom?" and so on. For acting out probable situations, participants can be given certain roles which will tax the leader's skill and ingenuity, roles such as "dominator," "obstructionist," "playboy," "conciliator," "initiator," and so forth. Or practice may be given in meeting group situations that commonly occur in an orientation class: an initial meeting, or a meeting in which role-playing is introduced for the first time, or a planning meeting. Such make-believe situations can give novice leaders some familiarity with handling group problems and give practiced leaders a chance to sharpen their skills as well as to contribute to the training of others.

Workshops or other training sessions should also give instruction and provide experience in the use of special devices such as role-playing, buzz sessions, evaluation methods, brainstorming, panels, and the case method. Each instructor should have a chance to practice role-playing and to gain the experience of actually participating in buzz sessions, brainstorming, panels, and case discussions. (Sample cases and evaluation sheets that could be used in such practice are included in the Appendix.)

Finally, a workshop should include a careful consideration of the art of individual counseling, with lecture, discussion, and role-playing being brought to bear on the matter.

The instructor's role as a general counselor to each of the students in his orientation class may be elucidated by lecture and discussion, with recommendations on how often he should see the student, what he can hope to accomplish, what should be his scope and his limits. Other problems that usually need illumination are the counselor's relationship to the parents (this may well vary with the institution); referral agencies and methods of referral (psychological services, vocational counselors, and so forth; the counselor's role in relation to other faculty (does he intercede, investigate, and so forth?); and the nature of the relationship between counselor and student.

Role-playing can be very useful in this portion of workshop activities. It gives the individual a controlled kind of practice in counseling, stimulates discussion, and can lead to a considerable amount of insight into methods and points of view toward counseling. Briefly stated cases or "situations" can be prepared in advance and acted out either before the whole group or simultaneously in several small groups.

Chapter

9.

INDIVIDUAL COUNSELING AS A SUPPLEMENT TO GROUP DEVELOPMENT

THE preceding chapters have described the orientation program in terms of the processes that occur in the group. There is, however, another important aspect of the program: the interaction of student and teacher in the course of individual counseling.

The formal requirements of the counseling aspect of orientation are very simple; every teacher is expected to meet briefly with each of his orientation students, his counselees, once every few weeks during the whole year. The actual length of the meeting may vary anywhere from five minutes to an hour, depending upon the needs of the student and the nature of the discussion.

Purposes of Individual Counseling

Individual conferences have to be looked at in the light of the overall purpose of orientation—to help the individual become more self-directing, self-educating.

For a person to approach the goal of self-direction requires that he gradually achieve independence of authority. One of the small steps that can be taken to accomplish this is to bring the student and teacher together in friendly informal talks in which the emphasis is on rapport, empathy and understanding.

Students can learn a great deal more from their teachers than just subject matter. The individual teacher can be not only a source of knowledge and an evaluator of skill; he can also be a source of support, a carrier of social values and mores, an object of friendship and an object of identification. Individual contacts help the student discover his teacher more as a warm human being and less as a remote authority figure.

There is a second purpose of the individual meetings between counselor and student.

If the conversation is warm and friendly, with no pressuring and with general acceptance of any thoughts that are expressed, if the teacher does not overwhelm the student with his own ideas or recommendations, it is almost certain that the student will eventually bring up any problems that may be bothering him. Problems which a student may feel he cannot raise in the group, he usually can express to his counselor.

For example, many college freshmen have difficulty studying and getting the most out of their assignments; many are shocked and unhappy at their first grades. These failures and personal failings are usually not discussed in the group until a rapport has begun to prevail, usually around mid-semester, but they are often brought to the counselor's attention much earlier through individual conferences.

In summary, the individual conference gives the student a chance to express ideas which he would be reluctant to express in a group or that he would like to explore further.

There is a third important function of the individual conference. Oftentimes in the course of private meetings, group members who have been quiet and apparently withdrawn, begin to present ideas and observations of great cogency and depth. It is important to encourage such a student to present his ideas and make his contributions to the group as well as in the private conferences. By increased participation in the group he will benefit not only himself but the other students as well.

A fourth important purpose of individual conferences is to insure there being at least one person on the faculty who knows each student well.

From time to time student problems arise which require knowledge of the student's background, his behavior, and potential if they are to be intelligently solved. The person most suited to help with the solution is the orientation teacher. At the end of the freshman year many students may be dropped, or are put on probation, or allowed to waver on the borderline. In many cases, the orientation teacher's evaluation of the student's progress, attitude, and potential is invaluable in arriving at a proper decision. For this purpose, each teacher is required to submit at the end of the year a written evaluation of each of his counselees which includes comments on the student's current performance and what might be expected of him in the future, his vocational aims and his personality traits. These reports are permanently filed with the student's official records and are available when any special problems come up.

The fifth function of the individual conferences is to serve as a referral service for maladjusted students.

In most cases, the counselor can handle student problems more or less adequately through exercising acceptance, friendliness, tact, and patience, and by helping the student to realize that the ultimate solution must be his own rather than the teacher's. The teacher can usually be more helpful by restating the problem for the student (reflecting), by helping him clarify his ideas, and by perhaps suggesting alternate ways of looking at an issue. When these approaches do not seem to help, or when the teacher feels that the type of problem presented is of such a nature that he cannot deal with it at all, it is wise and prudent tactfully to refer the student to competent professional help.

At many colleges, there is a Psychological Counseling Center available for such referrals; when it is not available, there are usually psychologists or psychiatrists in the college area who can be contacted. Although the total number of such referrals during any given year may be small, such counseling services should be available when they are needed.

The sixth and by no means least important purpose of the individual conference is to insure that each student entering college has one adviser to whom he can always turn during his freshman year. In the welter of new activities, responsibilities, and regulations, the beginning student often feels confused and at a loss. He may be concerned about anything from freshman hazing to the problem of how to get a loan. Knowing that there is one person always ready to see him and help him deal with any issue is a source of security and at the same time a morale-booster. The student feels that the college is concerned with him personally, even though he may be only one of a thousand entering students. And this fact will help to bring him closer to the college itself and make him more willing to identify with its traditions and its rules.

At the same time that the counselor is trying to help the

student in any way possible, he is also acting as a kind of liaison between the college and the student. The orientation teacher receives notices from time to time about freshman government and elections, special reading classes, help workshops, and general college regulations, information which he can pass along to his counselees. He also receives the results of tests which students take on entering college and can convey them at his discretion to individual students.

These six general purposes of individual conferences determine in large measure the function of the counselor: he listens, he encourages, he stimulates, he clarifies, he reflects, he refers, he questions, and he gives information.

Types of Problems

Problems that students present in the individual conferences may run the gamut of human issues. A listing, therefore, cannot be exhaustive, but can only focus on the major content areas of the discussions. These issues of concern to students can be grouped into five main areas: problems of fact, of study, of motivation, of personal difficulties, and vocation.

Problems of Fact. A common kind of problem, particularly at the beginning of the semester, simply reflect a need for factual data. Students want to know how to join a club or fraternity, or where the library is, or how they might get a part-time job on campus, or how they may drop a course. These are questions which the counselor can usually answer easily enough; generally such matters are explained in various official college publications.

A simple, direct answer is in most cases the simplest way to handle such questions. Frequently, however, it is well to consider whether it might not contribute more to the student's growth to suggest that he go and find the answer for himself. Students who are inclined to be very dependent may use such "problems" as a way of gratifying a dependent attachment toward the counselor, who should be keenly aware of this possibility in his relationship with his students. The basic principle that should guide his decisions is his desire to help the student develop his own self-directing attitudes and thereby help make him gradually more and more independent.

Although fact seeking questions may be numerous at first, they greatly decrease as familiarity with new surroundings and new regulations develops and as group members establish sufficient rapport to bring up such matters for group discussion.

One other important point should be recognized. There are some students who will use this kind of factual question as an introductory contact with the counselor, as a prelude to talking about more important personal problems. For example, a student may come to the counselor and say, "I want to know how I can change my course; can you help me?" If the teacher simply gives a factual answer to this question and thus, by implication, dismisses the student as well as the problem, a whole area concerning motivation may be left unexplored. On the other hand, if the student is invited to talk out his feelings concerning the proposed change, the counselor will gain an understanding of the kind of person he is. Furthermore, because the student will now see that the counselor is really interested in him as a person, there will be a corresponding gain in rapport.

Problems of Study. Once the specific factual questions have been taken care of, the most common problem is how to get the most out of study. Once the semester is well under way, discussions of study difficulties become more and more usual; they are almost always discussed first in the individual conferences and then, with a little encouragement, in the group. Almost everyone begins to describe some difficulty: "I can't seem to concentrate on my books; after ten or fifteen minutes my mind begins to wander." Or, "No matter where I study at home I can hear the TV or radio going, or my kid brother." Or, "I can study my history all right but I just don't seem to have any interest in biology, so I really never look at the book." Or, "Some of my buddies keep dropping in and ask me to go out for a beer. So I go." Or, "When I get to my room after work and stretch out on a couch to study, before I know it I'm asleep."

As can be surmised, there are many different reasons for the study difficulties students experience. The major ones might be roughly classified in the following way, although the list is by no means exhaustive:

(a) lack of knowledge of good study habits
(b) poor reading skills
(c) low motivation
(d) distractions
(e) excessive outside work

As the list implies, although study problems may be caused by specific lack of skills, they may also be connected with complex problems of motivation and personality. There is, of course, no universal solution for all study problems.

What, then, can be done? First, a sympathetic exploration of the student's conception (or diagnosis) of his own problem. One must recognize too, that there is likely to be more than a single aspect of the problem. For example, it is easy to find a student who has poor study habits and is also a slow reader, or one who has low motivation, and is also easily distracted.

If a student is a very slow reader, he may be referred to special classes, or at least be made aware of some of the conditions for better reading. If the student has poor study practices, there are many films, books and pamphlets which will help him learn better ones and which can be brought to his attention (see listing in the Appendix). If the amount of time devoted to outside work seems excessive, this problem should be discussed thoroughly and, if economically feasible, a reduction of working hours recommended. If distractions are plentiful at home, one might, for example suggest a greater use of the college library.

It is generally very useful to ask the student to describe *in detail* the conditions under which he studies. This includes such matters as the number of hours spent daily, the time of day, the place, the specific conditions, and so on. A thorough exploration will often give both the student and the teacher an awareness of the inadequacies in the student's study method.

Problems of Motivation. If the problem is one of low motivation, the solution is much more difficult. Here deep-seated attitudes and personality traits are likely to be involved. Not infrequently a student will suggest that he is doing poorly in his college work because he has lost interest. He may say that he started with great enthusiasm but the subjects have become boring and that he realizes they are not of much use to him. After all, why does a business major have to take biology or a language?

If the counselor does not try to answer the question as posed but rather encourages further comments on the matter, he will usually find that attitudes other than those directly expressed are involved.

He may discover, for example, that the first examination grades have just been returned in some course and that the student failed, or that the student finds his homework too difficult to do. *When the motivation of a student falls abruptly, it usually indicates an experience of failure.* It is wise for the counselor in such a situation to be a good listener, to allow the student to express his disappointment, and to try tactfully to support further efforts to succeed.

Related to this problem is the whole question of the purpose of college, and it is generally appropriate at this time to explore with the student some of his reasons for coming to college and particularly the *expectations* he had about college. Here especially one is likely to find that college has turned out to be far different from what the student had thought it would be. In such a case, it would be particularly appropriate to encourage the student to bring his questions into the group meeting. If, however, low motivation persists and is accompanied by strong feelings of worthlessness or depression, referral for psychological counseling may be necessary.

Sometimes a student will try to justify his low motivation by some rationalization. For example, he may complain that the material is impractical, or useless, or that the classes are too large or that the teacher is boring. Even when there may be an element of truth in such charges, they generally do not justify failing work or withdrawal.

In any event, the basic techniques of the counselor's art in the case of students with low or lessening motivation are to listen, reflect, and encourage.

Problems of Personal Difficulties. Occasionally, a student will reveal problems relating to some personal difficulty not immediately connected with his college work. For example, (and generally toward the middle or end of the semester), a student may describe difficulties which he has at home. He may not get along well with one or both of his parents and the difficulty may be increasing as the term progresses. Or a girl may reveal that her boy friend who is at an out-of-town college is always on her mind and that she can't concentrate on her work. Or a shy student tells how painfully difficult it is to approach someone of the opposite sex for a date.

In such situations the orientation teacher should recognize his own limitations. Here especially it is necessary that he maintain a non-evaluative attitude and not convey his own feeling that something the student is doing is right or wrong or good or bad. It is important to listen sympathetically, reflect the student's own ideas back to him (which will show him that you at least understand what he is trying to say), and, perhaps, suggest the possibility of talking about the problem in the group. You might bring to his attention the fact that many people have similar problems and that a mutual airing might contribute in some measure to a solution. Other than this, the less pressure put on the student with such problems, the better. But if, in the course of time, the problem does not seem to diminish, then at some point it becomes appropriate to suggest the possibility of psychological counseling.

Problems of Vocation. A source of concern to most college freshmen is the problem of choice of major and, by implication, of vocation. In many colleges, a major is expected to be chosen by the end of the sophomore year, yet many students have not decided or have decided only with reservations by this time. In addition, many students have not as yet even been exposed to a variety of courses such as sociology, psychology or geology which may turn out to be of sufficient interest to provide a major. It seems to us, then, that the orientation teacher's role as vocational adviser is largely one of counseling patience and pointing out the need for obtaining more information.

When discussing vocational plans with students, the teacher's role is usually limited to (a) making known to the students the results of any entrance tests he may have taken (such as the Kuder Preference Record), (b) interpreting these test results to the student, and (c) referring the student to other sources of information, including other departments of the college where he can obtain specific information on course curricula, books on specific vocations, and the vocational guidance counselor who is available on most college campuses.

Referral

Teachers sometimes find the problem of referral of a student for psychological counseling a difficult task. The major difficulty is that the student is likely to resent being told that he needs help. Although this possibility may never be entirely discounted, it may be minimized if the teacher proceeds with tact and understanding.

The situations which may necessitate referral will generally be of one of the following types:

(a) A student becomes aware of some marked personal difficulties in his relations to others, and may directly ask for help.

(b) A student finds the school situation increasingly difficult to deal with. His grades may be going down, his motivation failing, and he may report increasing inability to concentrate on his studies.

(c) A student begins to show unusual, or even bizarre behavior.

In the first case it is usually a simple matter to refer the student to a competent person. In cases of the second type the orientation teacher may feel that the approaching failure is incompatible with the student's potential, as indicated by his entrance examinations and impressions he has given in individual conferences. In such a case the teacher may gradually and tactfully raise the possibility that academic difficulties are sometimes related to problems or distractions that arise in the student's off-campus life. If the student easily accepts and elaborates on this theme, then the task of referral is made easier; if not, greater patience and a more gradual approach become necessary.

Basically, the orientation teacher points out to the student that if there are serious problems or difficulties on his mind that seem to be interfering with successful college work, they may be dealt with a little more adequately if he has a chance to talk it over with a specially trained, understanding person. He points out too, that such a service is provided by the college—in the Dean of Students Office, for example—and that the student is free to take advantage of it if he wishes. This approach leaves the choice and the responsibility entirely in the hands of the student and, in addition, does not make him feel pressured into going. It also tends to eliminate feelings of resentment which the student might feel if he were told outright that there seemed to be something wrong with him and that he should see a psychologist. In this kind of referral situation, especially, tact and patience are essential.

The third type of referral situation, where a student may show bizarre behavior, occurs very rarely. If it does appear, the counselor should try to get the student to see the psychologist or psychiatrist on campus as quickly as possible. If such a student recognizes that he has a serious problem the orientation counselor may telephone for an appointment immediately. If the student seems reluctant to recognize the seriousness of his behavior, then he should be gotten to the psychologist's office on some reasonable excuse. Tact and patience are necessary here also, but it is essential that such a student be placed in competent hands quickly.

Chapter

10.

IMPLICATIONS OF
GROUP-CENTERED LEADERSHIP
FOR OTHER TEACHING

THE schools and colleges in America today have assumed responsibilities far beyond those of their predecessors. In a more direct, self-conscious and deliberate way they are trying to provide a broad, character-building education, which includes not only intellectual attainment and vocational preparation but social adaptability as well. Important as individual initiative and isolated thinking may be, group skills are increasingly significant in modern life. It is also necessary to realize that there is no conflict between individual sensitivity and group expression; both are required, and, indeed, both can best be acquired together.

Orientation through group-centered leadership is one kind of approach to the fostering of social and intellectual skills along with personal responsibility. If our experiences over the past few years are a true index, this kind of orientation program reduces the barriers to communication and concomitant feelings of aloneness, gives the individual an immediate and personal taste of democracy in action—of respect for each individual and his contribution—and increases his opportunity to assess realistically the world and himself.

In addition to the effect orientation may have on the students who are involved in it directly, it also has other effects on the college community. It is the purpose of this chapter to note some of the implications of this truth.

What Are the Functions of a Teacher?

The answers which each of us give to the question of what are the functions of a teacher will determine in part our readiness and willingness to explore new teaching methods in our own classrooms.

Is the teacher a source of facts, a guide, a spur, a persuader, a mentor, an explainer, an administrator, an encourager? Or is he, as some psychologists have suggested,[1] an object of love or hate, an object of identification, a source of support, a carrier of mores and values, an evaluator and a counselor? Or, perhaps, is the teacher most or all of these things regardless of how he may actually interpret his function.

The variety of answers which may be given to such a question strongly suggests that the teacher does have multiple functions in any classroom, functions which are determined partly by the students and partly by the teacher's own intentions and skills.

The teacher who has acquired the skills necessary for leading orientation groups increases his readiness to accept and his ability to carry out these multiple teaching roles. A teacher may or may not decide to use the procedures of orientation in another class, but an awareness of these procedures will at least assure their being available if he has occasion to use them. Further, the increased sensitivity to

---

[1] S. Scheidlinger, "Should Teachers Be Group Therapists?" *Progressive Education,* 1955, 32, 70-74.

personal feelings and interactions in a group which a teacher gains through participation in an orientation program, increases his ability to adapt to new situations and to assume new roles when new situations demand that he do so. To recruit orientation leaders from the general faculty is, we believe, as important to improved teaching of other subjects as it is to the success of the orientation program itself.

Lecture versus Discussion

In recent years there have been many criticisms leveled at the teaching approach which uses lectures exclusively. Its critics contend that it offers the professor all the educative activity, while lulling the students into passivity. The students learn to take lecture notes, but not to think problems through for themselves.

In any case, there is little question that recent years have seen a trend toward greater freedom of discussion in American classrooms and a greater reliance on "discussion methods." This trend undoubtedly stems from the feeling that the student should shoulder more of the responsibility for his own education, for he will thus be more likely to develop sustained motivation, a central element in education. Technical competence in a subject is not enough; the student must learn how to acquire new knowledge on his own, to appraise it, and to use it creatively. As Elbert Hubbard once put it, "The object of teaching a child is to enable him to get along without his teacher."

Professor Gibb, in a study at the University of Colorado, has contended that the typical college classroom is "content-oriented and teacher-oriented. The students tended to be passive or neutral listeners, to raise occasional questions, to criticize the activities of the classrooms outside of class in a person-oriented rather than a goal-oriented way, to accept for normal purposes the goals of the teacher, and the teacher's prerogative to set goals and give assignments . . . to resent being placed in active roles, to look upon organization, evaluation, and problem formulation as the teacher's job."

These observations led Professor Gibb to develop an experimental "participative-action" group in a first course in psychology. The class members were allowed, within certain very wide but defined limits, to make all the decisions in the course relating to formulation of goals, specific content requirements, general classroom activities, and the choice of criteria for grades. The instructor trained them in various methods of group actions, such as role playing and evaluation procedures.

Objective and essay tests, scored by independent observers, indicated a slight superiority for the experimental classes as compared with classes taught in the usual way. The experimental groups also were much higher on such variables as self-insight, quality of discussion and attitudes toward science.[2]

It is not necessarily recommended that all courses be developed in just this way but the significant finding here is that these group discussion procedures resulted in just as efficient content learning as the more traditional methods. In addition, there was a gain in social skills and insights.

[2] J. R. Gibb, "The 'Participative-action' Group in the First Course in Psychology." And L. M. Gibb and J. R. Gibb, "Effects of the Use of 'Participative-action' Groups in General Psychology." Delivered at the American Psychological Association meeting September 1952.

Guides for Classroom Participation

Although every teacher must adapt group methods to fit both his subject area and his personality, a few general principles may be suggested:

1. Communication between students and teachers is reciprocal and relatively free. Questions, comments, and discussion are welcome.
2. The goals and limits of the class are clear. Student background and participation are considered in goal setting.
3. The classroom atmosphere is friendly, accepting, but realistic.
4. The teacher encourages the individual to take increasing responsibility for his own development.
5. The teacher tries to be flexible in his methods of operation and is sensitive to group variations in mood and interest.
6. The teacher recognizes that each member of the class is an actual or potential resource person whose experiences and special skills may contribute to the intellectual and social development of the group.
7. The teacher recognizes the values of demonstrations and individual participation in class activities. The opportunity to try out and practice new skills and attitudes is of central importance.
8. The teacher recognizes the need to be alert to the effects his own behavior may have on others. "Feedback" can be obtained by means of class discussions, individual conferences, questionnaires, tests, formal evaluations, and tape recordings.

Need for Evaluation

How well can a teacher judge his degree of success in the process of educating students? There are, of course, many books which can be helpful in describing evaluation forms to be completed by students. But such forms will not tell the whole story. The type of evaluation used for adult education, however, is particularly significant, since adult education, is likely to lack coercive elements. What the adult learner needs to know is whether or not his learning has effected a change in him. He asks questions of the following kind in evaluating a course of study:

(a) Has it increased my useable fund of reliable information?

(b) Have I changed my vocabulary? Can I use new concepts?

(c) Have I acquired new skills?

(d) Have I learned how to make reliable generalizations?

(e) Have I learned how to sort out the moral ingredients in the various situations considered here?

(f) Have I altered any attitudes?

These kinds of changes are more likely to occur when a teacher utilizes the general principles of the group method. And these changes do tend to occur in orientation classes with group-centered leadership.

Some Large-Group Teaching Aids

One approach is to break up large groups into committees of eight or ten each for the discussion of particular issues, each committee under a rotating student chairman. This procedure, in conjunction with formal lectures, seems to create greater subject interest and to generate motivation for further library research.

Another device is the use of buzz groups. The instructor may pose a question and divide an entire large group into small groups of five or six each for a few minutes to discuss a question or respond to it in some way. A recorder from each subgroup will then report to the entire class the gist of its deliberations, which the instructor may in turn note on the blackboard. This device tremendously increases student interaction and individual involvement in large classes.

Panel discussions by groups of six or eight specially prepared students are often exciting and productive of group discussion. Forums can be used in very much the same way.

Even role playing can be used with large groups. Norman Maier writes of a development which he calls "audience role playing." [3] The teacher introduces by a lecture or group discussion some problem or issue in which feelings or attitudes influence a person's behavior: for example, what are the factors that influence the attitudes of employees toward a company? The audience is then asked to imagine themselves in the role of workers (or of management) in a dispute. The teacher can then read the details of some specific issue and get reactions from the audience from the point of view of the role they have adopted. These reactions may be obtained by questionnaires, story-completion tests, or by the use of buzz groups. Through role playing, an audience (or class) may be helped to see situations as if they were actually involved in them. As a result they understand more clearly why certain methods fail and others work.

[3] *Principles of Human Relations,* New York, Wiley, 1952, p. 157.

These few suggestions are only given in order to set the teacher thinking about the possible application of typical Orientation procedures to other college classrooms. With imagination, other combinations will be found.

Barriers to Change

Many of these ideas are not particularly new. How is it that they are not in much wider use? What are the barriers that keep us from trying new teaching techniques? One reason is simply that effort is needed to change. A person who has learned to teach in one way finds that it takes effort to learn new approaches and additional effort to put them into effect. Only if an instructor feels there is good reason to change and is encouraged to do so is it likely that he will try.

A second barrier is fear of failure. Some teachers may be convinced of the value of buzz groups, for example, and yet be afraid to try them because unexpected things may occur.

A third factor preventing change is the fear of loss of status. There is satisfaction in having reached a position of respect for one's knowledge. If the teacher tries a new technique and it does not work very well, the students may feel that he is not sure of what he is doing. In a discussion group, the teacher becomes more a resource person than an authority figure *per se;* he has to achieve "earned" authority on the basis of his knowledge as well as "uncarned" authority on the basis of his position. This is sometimes considered a drawback.

Another barrier to change is fear of unfavorable reactions from colleagues. Even when a new teaching method is successful the instructor is likely to feel that other professors think that he is deserting the tried and true academic traditions.[4] Acceptance from one's peers is important for college professors as well as others.

Dealing with Barriers

How can these barriers be dealt with? The first and most important way of dealing with these obstacles to change is to be sure of the reasons for trying a new technique. If the new ventures seem consistent with our goals of education, once they have been thought through, then the chances of trying them are greatly increased.

A second support for change is group acceptance. When our colleagues are sympathetic to these new ideas and have successfully used them there is a much greater impetus to try them ourselves. This is one of the reasons why teacher-training programs and in-service training programs are so important. The exchange of ideas and discussion of experiences among teachers does a great deal to increase the tendency to experiment with new techniques and ideas.

Such programs, in addition, give the teacher a chance to experiment directly with and become personally involved with these new group techniques.

And finally, an important source of support for change is the sense of satisfaction one derives when the technique is first tried and it works well. This means that it should be tried in a class or a group where good relations have already been set up or where the instructor feels he is most likely to be successful. In some cases it may even be worthwhile to

[4] See W. J. McKeachie, "Improving Your Teaching," in *How to Teach Adults*, Adult Education Association, 1955.

ask for volunteers to join a special section of the class which will experiment with a new learning method.

In Conclusion

Orientation Through Group Development has important implications for other college teaching. It provides a student-centered philosophy of education which has relevance to other types of classes; it provides training in new skills—group discussion leadership, and special devices for facilitating interaction—which may be used in other types of situations; and it helps the teacher develop increased sensitivity to his relations with others.

To make the most of these opportunities, teachers must be willing to accept the challenge of change. In the words of Edwin Fred, President of the University of Wisconsin, "College professors must be willing to experiment. They must be imaginative, not thinking of education in terms of hours, credits, grades and patterns of courses. They must infuse the entire campus life with experience meaningful to each student, sending him out as an able, poised service-minded, socially-responsible member of a community. Consequently, university teaching should be directed to arousing curiosity and impelling the student to find answers for himself."

Appendix

1. *Selected list of books for the orientation teacher*
2. *Sources for booklets and pamphlets*
3. *Occupational information*
4. *Selected listing of film sources*
5. *List of workshops for summer training*
6. *A sample case prepared for discussion purposes: Case of Peter Baxter*
7. *Letter to parents*
8. *End-of-year report on counselees*
9. *In-service training outline*
10. *Evaluation forms*
11. *Mid-year report of orientation counselors*
12. *Freshman counseling record*
13. *Synopsis of topics for orientation class*

1. SELECTED LIST OF BOOKS FOR THE ORIENTATION TEACHER

Cantor, Nathaniel   *Dynamics of Learning,* Foster & Stewart, Buffalo, New York, 1950.

Haiman, Franklyn S.   *Group Leadership and Democratic Action,* Houghton Mifflin, New York, 1950.

Hoffmann, R. W. and Plutchik, R.   *Controversy,* G. P. Putnam's Sons, New York, 1959.

Klein, Alan F.   *Role Playing in Leadership Training and Group Problem Solving,* Association Press, New York, 1956.

Thelen, Herbert A.   *Dynamics of Groups at Work,* University of Chicago Press, 1954.

Educator's Washington Dispatch   *Portfolio of College Teaching Techniques,* 1950 to present.

Hall, D. M.   *The Dynamics of Group Discussion,* Interstate, Danville, Illinois, 1950.

Frank, Lawrence K.   *How to Be a Modern Leader,* Association Press, New York, 1954.

Lasker, Bruno   *Democracy Through Discussion,* New York, Wilson, 1949.

Rogers, Carl R.   *Becoming a Person,* Available from Hogg Foundation for Mental Hygiene, The University of Texas, 1954.

Driver, Helen I., *et al.* *Counseling and Learning Through Small-Group Discussion,* Monona Publications, Madison, Wisconsin, 1958.

2. SOURCES FOR BOOKLETS AND PAMPHLETS

The magazine *Adult Leadership,* published monthly by the Adult Education Association, regularly includes many useful articles on adult education and human relations problems.

The Anti-Defamation League of B'nai B'rith publishes many booklets on various aspects of human relations. For an annotated bibliography of over one hundred titles write to the League at 515 Madison Avenue, New York 22, N. Y.

The National Conference of Christians and Jews publishes many pamphlets. A list of publications may be obtained by writing them at 381 Fourth Avenue, New York 16, N. Y.

The Center for the Study of Liberal Education for Adults, 940 East 58th Street, Chicago 37, Illinois, publishes many thoughtful reports and essays dealing with educational problems.

3. OCCUPATIONAL INFORMATION

The *Occupational Outlook Handbook* can be obtained from The Superintendent of Documents, U. S. Government Printing Office, Washington 25, D. C. Short reprints describing particular occupations can also be obtained from this source.

The New York Life Insurance Company, 51 Madison Avenue, New York 10, N. Y., has prepared short booklets describing a wide variety of occupations. These are free. This company has also compiled a bibliography of recent occupational literature called a *Guide to Career Information, Harper,* New York, 1957.

A useful source book is *Occupational Information,* by Carroll L. Shartle, Prentice-Hall, New York, 1952.

The Institute for Research, 537 South Dearborn Street, Chicago 5, Illinois, publishes "Careers Research Monographs" which survey over 1800 distinct types of jobs.

4. SELECTED LISTING OF FILM SOURCES

The following sources provide listings of films which may be useful for Orientation groups:

ADL: Freedom Library. Anti-Defamation League of B'nai B'rith, 515 Madison Avenue, New York 10, N. Y.

Christian Friends Bulletin, Vol. 12, No. 1: Programming for Democracy. Anti-Defamation League of B'nai B'rith, 212 Fifth Avenue, New York 10, N. Y.

Films in Psychiatry, Psychology and Mental Health. Health Education Council, No. 10 Downing St., New York 14, N. Y.

16 mm Films in Health, Education and Welfare. International Film Bureau, 57 East Jackson Blvd., Chicago 4, Illinois.

Guide to Films in Human Relations. Department of Audio-Visual Instruction, National Education Association, 1201 Sixteenth St. N.W., Washington 6, D. C.

Human Relations and Audio-Visual Materials. The National Conference of Christians and Jews, 43 West 57th St., New York 19, New York.

Mental Health Motion Pictures. Public Health Service Publication, Superintendent of Documents, U. S. Government Printing Office, Washington 25, D. C.

Mental Health Publications and Audio-Visual Aids. The National Association for Mental Health, 1790 Broadway, New York 19, New York.

Mental Mechanisms Series and the *What Do You Think?* *Series,* National Film Board of Canada, Canada House, 680 Fifth Avenue, New York 19, New York.

Selected Films for World Understanding. Wendell W. Williams, Audio-Visual Center, Division of Adult Education and Public Services, Indiana University, Bloomington, Indiana.

Selected List of Human Relations Films. Film Division of the American Jewish Committee, 386 Fourth Avenue, New York 16, New York.

5. LIST OF WORKSHOPS FOR SUMMER TRAINING

There are a large number of summer workshops useful for improving human relations skills. A few are listed below with the address from which information may be obtained.

National Conference of Christians and Jews Workshops and Seminars in Human Relations and Intergroup Education, NCCJ, Commission on Educational Organizations, 381 Fourth Ave., New York 16, N. Y.

National Training Laboratory in Group Development, NTLGD, 1201 Sixteenth St. N.W., Washington 6, D. C.

Lisle Fellowship, Inc., DeWitt Baldwin, Director, 294 South State St., Ann Arbor, Michigan

Role of Communications in Human Relations, Director of Summer Session, University of Pittsburgh, Pittsburgh, Penna.

Saskatchewan Institute in Group Development, Adult Education Division, 1100 Broad Street, Regina, Sask., Canada

Work Conference on the Role of the Consultant, Teachers College, Columbia University, New York 27, N. Y.

Boston University Workshop in Improving Human Relations, Conference Center, North Andover, Mass.

Kenneth D. Benne, Director, Boston University, Human Relations Center, 308 Bay State Road, Boston 15, Mass.

Midwest Workshop in Community Human Relations, Mrs. Bettie Sarchet, University College, 19 South LaSalle St., Chicago 3, Illinois

Workshop in the Techniques of Counseling, Mrs. Leslie F. Kimmell, American Institute of Family Relations, 5287 Sunset Boulevard, Los Angeles 27, California

Western Training Laboratory in Group Development, University Extension, University of California, Los Angeles 24, Calif.

Midwest Training Center in Human Relations, Edward F. Memmott, Ex. Sec'y, MTC, Urbana Junior College, Urbana, Ohio

Southwest Human Relations Training Laboratory, HRTL, Dept. of Psychology, University of Texas, Austin, Texas

Pacific Northwest Laboratory in Group Development, Betty Dimmitt, Office of Short Courses & Conferences, University of Washington, Seattle 5, Washington

A SAMPLE CASE PREPARED FOR DISCUSSION PURPOSES

6. CASE OF PETER BAXTER

Harbor College, where Peter Baxter is a junior, enrolls each year about a thousand full-time students and fifteen hundred part-time (evening) students. It is a young college, founded in 1910, but it has an able faculty, a good administration, and a fiscal policy that keeps it in the black but does not allow too many frills and luxuries.

The President of Harbor is concerned primarily with fund raising and public relations. The Vice President devotes his time primarily to plant development. The Dean of the Faculty concerns himself with curriculum development, faculty welfare, and co-ordination of departmental business and personnel. The Provost supervises and co-ordinates the work of the Dean of the Faculty, Dean of Students, Registrar, and Dean of Admissions.

Student Personnel administration consists of a Dean of Students, to whom report the Dean of Men, the Dean of Women, the Director of Student Activities, and the Psychological Counselor. The Dean of Students Office is responsible for discipline, counseling, and all co-curricular activities except intercollegiate athletics.

The Director of Athletics reports directly to the Provost but also has the ear of the President. The Dean of Students has no jurisdiction in the athletic or physical education area.

Although there is a well organized student government program at Harbor, the Administration reserves the right to make ultimate decisions, and to modify or reverse decisions made by the students. The students do not have a voice in the running of the College.

For several years now the faculty, the student body, and the administration have been perturbed by what they view as an excessive amount of cheating among the students, on exams, quizzes, term papers, themes, etc. This has been the only problem of any proportion at Harbor for the last three or four years. It seems to occur more among the men than among the women, or at least more men get caught.

The honor system has been talked of many times, but so far has not been tried. Many feel that the lack of integration among the student body, since Harbor is a commuter's college and has no dormitories, would doom the honor system to failure and the situation would be worse than it now is. There has also been talk of making a concerted drive on cheating and punishing offenders severely and inexorably. In the Dean of Students Office there are at least two views: (1) the Dean of Students believes that an individual caught cheating is more in need of counseling than punishment; (2) the Dean of Men feels that students should be held strictly accountable for their deeds and if an individual is caught cheating he should get the limit of the law.

A combined student-faculty board has been set up to handle honor violations. This consists of three students, the Dean of the Faculty, the Dean of Students or his representative, the chairman of the department in which the offense has occurred, and a faculty member from the Student Conduct Committee (a standing committee of the faculty). When an offense is tried, the faculty member involved sits with the Board without a vote. Cases are referred first to the Dean of Students Office and then by the Dean to the Honor Board. The following rules are printed in the student handbook:

"Discipline in instances of academic dishonesty is administered in the following manner:

A. Cases of major dishonesty: plagiarism on term papers, cheating on hour examinations, mid-term or final examinations, or repeated dishonesty of any kind.

1. All cases are to be reported to the Dean of Students.

2. After investigation and consultation with the person or persons involved, the Dean of Students presents the case to the Honor Board, composed of the Dean of Faculty, the Dean of Students or his representative, a member of Student Conduct Committee, the departmental chairman, the instructor of the course in which the offense occurred, and those students chosen to serve as representatives of the student body. Appropriate action shall be determined by at least a majority vote of the Board.

3. Penalties:

   a. First offense: "F" final grade in the course.
   b. Second offense: dishonorable dismissal from the College.
   c. Variations from the above penalties may be made at the discretion of the committee.
   d. Offenses and penalties shall be published in the Harbor Cry. Names of persons and courses will not be published.
   c. A record of each offense and penalty shall be inserted on the student's history sheet and on the personal record card of the student involved. Such records will be confidential.

B. Cases of minor dishonesty: Plagiarism (first offense) on book report or weekly theme; cheating (first offense) on daily quiz or test.

1. Handled in its entirety by the instructor in whose course the offense occurred.

2. A written report of the offense and the penalty imposed shall be made by the instructor to the Dean of Students who will attach a report to the student's personal record card. Notation will not be made on the student's history sheet.

3. Such offenses and penalties shall be treated strictly confidential by the Dean of Students and the instructor involved.

It is the sincere hope of the students and the faculty that this plan will be a step toward a complete honor system, whereby each student will be responsible for his own honesty and general campus conduct."

At the time that the offense occurred in which Peter Baxter was involved, the Dean of Students, Dean Good, was away for a week on a belated vacation. He was visiting his son, who was a sophomore at Fairview College. Dean Good's son, incidentally, had been a star athlete in high school, but Dean Good had sent him to a college at which there were no intercollegiate athletics.

Peter Baxter had been apprehended in a plagiarism offense involving a term paper in Political Science, his major. The teacher, Professor White, had detected a familiarity in certain parts of the paper, had found that approximately half of the paper had been plagiarized from an article in a political science journal, and confronting Peter Baxter with the proof, had received a confession. After his confession, Peter became sullen and incommunicative, and Professor White referred the case to the Dean of Students' Office, where it was received and studied by Dean Law (the Dean of Men), in Dean Good's absence. Dean Law called Peter Baxter in and Peter reiterated his confession but again clammed up on further questioning. Dean Law made the necessary arrangement to convene the Honor Board two days following.

The offense occurred on March 3 and was tried by the Honor Board on March 6. The tone of the meeting was vindictive from the start, with the three students and Dean Law advocating the maximum penalty. A motion that Peter Baxter be dropped from the College was brought to a secret ballot and prevailed 4 to 3. Dean Law later admitted that he voted in favor of the motion.

Peter Baxter was informed by Dean Law of the action taken, and was told that he would receive an official letter from Dean Good dropping him from the College as soon as the Dean returned.

When Dean Good returned to his desk the following Monday he found that he had an appointment at ten o'clock with Peter Baxter. Dean Law spent a half hour with him, starting at nine o'clock, briefing him on the events that had led to Peter Baxter's desire for an appointment. Dean Good spent the next half hour looking through Peter Baxter's personal file, which included the high school record, letters of recommendation from principal and high school teachers, a neatly filled-out application blank, an activities report, and a very perceptive counseling report from Peter's Orientation teacher, who had also been his personal counselor during Peter's freshman year. Following are some of the things that Dean Good learned.

Peter came from a family of moderate means. Both parents' highest education had been four years of high school. He had no brothers but had a sister who had been graduated two years ago from college *cum laude,* and who was now working for TIME, Inc. He had an average high school record, an aptitude test record that indicated only average ability, and several testimonials to his sincerity, conscientiousness, and good character. He had been captain of his high school football team. His college grades showed him to be in danger of probation. He had not been able to make the varsity football team until his junior year, but in that year had done an outstanding job as an end. A newspaper clipping in his docket showed a picture of Peter with a story emphasizing the probability that Peter would have his greatest year next year and that Harbor would probably have its greatest football team in years. The counselor's report indicated that Peter was under a good deal of pressure at home, from his father to do well in football and from his mother to do well in his courses. Peter had an on-campus job that took 15 hours per week for which he received $1 an hour. He had a full-tuition scholarship that had started in the second semester of his junior year. (The condition for maintaining such a scholarship was that he stay off probation.) He also worked every summer both to help earn his college expenses and to help the family budget.

Dean Good had time to make a few phone calls before Peter came in. The Dean of the Faculty thought the penalty too harsh; Professor White felt that he should merely receive an F in the course; the chairman of the Political Science department thought that if Dean Good had been at the Board meeting the outcome would have been different.

Before Peter came in, the football coach telephoned to make a plea for a reversal of the judgment. "This boy," said the Coach, "has done a lot of good for Harbor, and a little mistake like this just doesn't merit such drastic punishment. I'm not thinking of my team, I'm thinking of the boy primarily, but just the same if we lose him it ruins the season and ruins all the good public relations that Harbor would get from the kind of season we could expect if Baxter stayed and played. Give him another chance; he's worth it to the College. I talked with the President about it and he thinks pretty much the same way."

(It should be noted that 12 of the thirty-six men on the Harbor football squad had full-tuition scholarships and 16 others had part-tuition scholarships.)

Dean Good had time for one more call before seeing Peter. This was to Frank Kotowski, one of the student members of the Honor Board, who was also Managing Editor of the Harbor CRY, the weekly student newspaper. Frank said that the three student members of the Board were solid in their opinion that the judgment was just, that it would not only be a good lesson for Peter Baxter but would also show the other students that stern action would be taken against cheating no matter who the offender was. This was a lesson, Frank said, that the Harbor student body badly needed. He said that the athletes of the College were notorious for their disregard of the honor regulations and other rules, and that Peter Baxter's offense was typical rather than out of the ordinary. Frank added that he had written an editorial praising the Board for its action, and that he would feel obliged to write one condemning any reversal or modification of the penalty. Dean Good, as usual, was impressed by Frank's forthrightness, honesty, and clear-headed analysis of the situation, but he was also apprehensive because of his awareness of Frank's well-nigh unshakable obstinacy.

A moment later Peter Baxter came in and said, "My father wanted to come with me, but I told him if I couldn't come to see you alone I wouldn't come at all."

7. LETTER TO PARENTS

To the Parents of Hofstra College Freshmen:

Approximately thirty faculty members have been chosen to act as advisors to the members of the freshman class at Hofstra College. During the first semester these counselors see the students individually for half-hour sessions about once every two weeks and meet them in groups of fifteen or twenty for an hour session twice a week.

This program of individual and group counseling is called Freshman Orientation and is designed to help your son and daughter make the necessary academic, social, and personal adjustment to college.

_____ has been named as _____

Orientation Counselor for the present academic year. This counselor will have a close personal relationship with each of the fifteen freshmen in his charge and will know each one of them better, probably, than anyone else in the College.

We have found that the counseling assistance given through Orientation can play a large part in the academic success and the personal happiness of beginning students at Hofstra. I hope that all parents will encourage their sons and daughters at Hofstra to take advantage of the services available to them through the Orientation Program.

You, as a parent, are free to get in touch with the counselor named above, either by phone, by letter, or by a personal visit to the College. If you prefer to get in touch with me and let me help you to make contact with the counselor, I shall be happy to hear from you.

Sincerely yours,

Randall W. Hoffmann
Dean of Students

P.S. A description of the Orientation Program at Hofstra College appears below.

Freshman Orientation at Hofstra

When young men and women start their college careers at Hofstra, they are usually at a stage of life characterized by (1) a desire to be independent of parental control, (2) a somewhat unrealistic notion of their ability to cope with life's problems, great or small, and (3) a tendency to feel reluctant to seek out help when they need it.

Here at Hofstra we realize that such attitudes can make life somewhat difficult, and we have tried to set up a safeguard against them. We know that many young men and women of eighteen are not yet completely ready for independence, and that they are not able alone to cope with all of life's problems. We also know that when a counseling service becomes an automatic part of their freshman program they do not feel hesitant to take advantage of it.

Hofstra College has set up just such a counseling service— called Orientation—in which all freshmen are required to enroll for the first semester and for which they receive college credit toward the requirements for graduation. Each student becomes a member of a small group which meets with the counselor for two hours each week, at which time the student has the opportunity of learning such skills as study habits and techniques, notetaking, report writing, and time budgeting. If his psychological tests show that he is having difficulty with reading, he is assigned to Orientation 1, which combines all the features described herein with intensive training in reading. This training will stand the student in good stead all through his college career.

At the group meetings he also can learn the place of extracurricular activities in the college picture, can bring up, and have discussed, his problems of vocational choice, can add to his knowledge of social usage and to his skill in human relations. In addition to all this he can, in the group or in individual conferences with his counselor, give voice to whatever personal problems he may have and with the guidance of the counselor approach a solution for some of these problems.

These counselors are selected for their warm interest in students as persons, for their knowledge of the academic and extracurricular organization of the College, and for the wisdom they can bring to bear on the problems of young people. They give generously of their time and energy. Their purpose, however, is not to force unwilling students to work, neither is it to guarantee that inferior students will succeed, nor is it to do for the student what the student should do for himself. Rather their purpose is to usher the student toward an acceptance of his responsibility to himself and society, to help him learn how to handle the freedom and independence he is trying to achieve, and finally to help him learn how to make the most out of college and how to let college make the most out of him.

These aims cannot be realized without the help of the parents. You can supplement and reinforce the work of the Orientation Counselor in several ways:

1. By encouraging your son or daughter to make and keep a close, friendly relationship with the Orientation Counselor.
2. By encouraging regular hours of study. (It should be remembered that college is a full-time job and that a student taking a normal program would find it necessary to spend about four hours per day, seven days a week, in study and preparation.)
3. By a quiet but insistent emphasis on the fact that achievement in the other important aspects of college life is meaningless without success in the academic subjects.

The Dean of Students Office

When an Orientation Counselor is presented with problems that require specialized attention, he has available the counseling services of the Dean of Students Office. Students are referred to this office who are having more than the usual difficulties in personal and social adjustment, in finding their vocational objectives, in acquiring the skills necessary for scholastic achievement, and the like.

The Dean of Students Office is staffed by competent counselors, is equipped to get at the root of most difficulties encountered by college students, and is ready to help any student in working out his personal problems. Parents should feel free to telephone, write, or visit the Dean of Students Office for information about the College or for help in understanding the problems confronting their son or daughter at Hofstra. For your convenience the personnel of the Dean of Students Office is named below. (Then follows the names of the Dean, Associate Dean, Assistant Dean, Director of Testing, Vocational Counselor, Co-ordinator of Student Activities, Psychological Counselor, Counseling Psychologist, and Orientation Counselors.)

Hofstra College   Hempstead, New York   IVanhoe 9-7000

8. END-OF-YEAR REPORT ON COUNSELEES

Counselee: Jane Doe
Counselor: Dr. Fredericks

May 28, 19—

Jane did quite well during her first semester and received an "A" in Social Science 1, three "B's" in Geology 1, History 3 and Orientation 3, and a "C" in English 1.

She expressed considerable disappointment in her performance in English 1, since she was planning on majoring in this area. Accordingly, she began to explore the possibility of becoming an education major and discussed this with me.

During our discussion she further stated that she is really less interested in public school teaching, and that she would like to consider advertising or public relations as her vocational objective. I felt that this was another possibility and encouraged her to explore this more fully. However, I suspect that her stronger interest is still in English, but that she is fearful of doing inadequately in this subject and has allowed her present grade to influence the direction of her choice. I suggested further testing and vocational guidance from Mr. Masten, which she agreed to pursue.

Jane contributed to orientation discussion and had a good relationship with the other students. She was relatively more mature than many of the other students in her class and helped them focus upon meaningful issues. With respect to co-curricular activities, she is presently pledging a sorority.

Once Jane clarifies her major, I am certain she will do superior college work and make a contribution to campus activities.

Counselee: John Doe
Counselor: P. J. Murphy

May 22, 19—

John received three "C's" in Social Science 1, Orientation 3, MST. In his other courses (English 1, History 1, and Geology 1) he received "D's".

Although John's entrance exam scores suggest that he has the ability for doing very good college work, he is lacking in self-direction. He appears to be under certain pressures from his parents to attend college and is also considerably indulged by them. In the past he has attended private schools and seems to have the feeling that "things will be done for him" when he gets into academic difficulty.

John participated in Orientation discussions but his immature attitude would sometimes cause the group to become sidetracked. Nevertheless he was accepted by other group members.

John still tends to be undecided about his major. Further testing and vocational guidance have been recommended. I feel a clarification of his vocational objective is extremely important in order to motivate him to perform more adequately.

Counselee: Russell Smith
Counselor: Dr. Black

September 9, 19—

Russell completed only two courses during his first semester and received "C's" in both English 1 and Social Science 1. He received "A's" in Geology 1, History 1 and "Inc." in Orientation. He withdrew from Hofstra in January, 1958.

It is not surprising that Russell dropped out of college because he seemed to lack motivation and did not take his work very seriously. The attitude and views he expressed in orientation class reflect an individual who is relatively immature. Although he was cooperative during our individual meetings, he did not discuss his plans to leave college with me, so that his reasons for doing so are unclear at this time.

Russell was rather ineffective in group discussions, and the other group members did not take him very seriously. Perhaps this interval away from an academic setting will help him clarify his goals and purpose in life.

Counselee: Albert Olson
Counselor: Miss E. Doyle

June 1, 19—

Al started out with an expressed interest in pre-law. However, it became clear through his participation in orientation class discussions that, although he has some interesting and creative ideas, he is not very articulate. Furthermore, despite his many contributions to the group discussions, I do not believe he was fully "appreciated" by other group members for two reasons. First, Al tends to be more individualistic than his peers and less of a conformist. Secondly, a strong interest in the arts created somewhat of a gap between him and the other students who frequently did not know the author or poet he would refer to. Nonetheless, he did have an important role insofar as he presented different sides of an issue for exploration and evaluation.

During the current semester, it became clear to him that he is less inclined toward legal work and has a strong interest in fine arts. Although he did an adequate job during his first semester and received two "B's" in Social Science 1 and Orientation 3, two "C's" in English 1 and History 1 and a "D" in Geology 1, he reports that he is not doing as well this semester. His decline in performance is undoubtedly related to his plans to leave college after this semester.

I encouraged him to evaluate the alternatives and to inspect the role of a college education in relation to his interests in writing and painting. Although he has not reversed his decision to leave college, he seemed more inclined to think of continuing college at some future date. I believe he will receive greater satisfaction from his work in art, and think this is a good choice for a major field of study.

9. IN-SERVICE TRAINING OUTLINE

FIRST DAY

Time	*Assignment*
9:00	Introduction to Workshop
9:25– 9:45	General explanation of Orientation
9:45–10:15	Practice initial meeting of class
10:15–10:30	Discussion of initial meeting (in small groups)
10:30–10:45	Coffee break
10:45–12:00	Explanation and demonstration of special devices
12:00– 1:00	Lunch
1:00– 2:15	Practice typical discussion
	(Hoffmann, Kronovet, Plutchik, will each take a group, give the group a topic, and lead a discussion. Then other members of each group will try leading it.)
2:15– 3:00	Total group discussion of leadership observed.

Assignment for tomorrow: mimeographed copies of "The Job of the Small-Group Leader."

SECOND DAY

9:00– 9:45	Lecture on leadership techniques and group behavior
9:45–10:00	Coffee break
10:00–10:20	Personal Counseling (Role-played)
	1. Initial counseling session

152

2. Typical counseling session
3. Referral type

10:20–10:50   Practice role playing of personal counseling.
              Break up into small groups
10:50–11:15   Psychological, vocational, and placement services
11:15–12:00   Film followed by discussion
12:00– 1:00   Lunch
 1:00– 2:00   Evaluation and questions

10. EVALUATION FORM

ORIENTATION

DATE_____

1. How satisfactory was today's meeting?

| | | | | |
| no good | mediocre | all right | good | excellent |

2. How clearly did we know what we were trying to do?

| | | | |
| clear to the last detail | some things clear | all confused |

3. How important were the problems we discussed?

| | | | |
| trivial, unrealistic problems | important but not our real concern | vital, central to our operation |

4. How much did we learn?

| | | | |
| a great deal | something | nothing |

5. Were we able to stick to our topics?

| | | | |
| very well | fairly well | not at all |

6. Amount of participation in group:

| | | | |
| everybody | half the group | one or two people |

7. How did we express our feelings?

directly, impulsively	readily, but only in connection with our tasks	inhibited, suppressed, or bottled up

8. How cooperatively did we work?

every man for himself; riding his own hobby	listened; some alignments of interest	we understood and built on each other's contributions

9. How energetic did the group seem?

bored, slow, apathetic listless	sober, contemplative	excited, very active tempo

10. How did we feel toward one another?

friendly, feeling of intimacy	each supported by some, not by others	strangers; remote from each other

11. How tense was the meeting?

completely relaxed, easy	some anxiety. problems	extremely tense

12. How would you describe the feeling in this meeting:
    (Place 1 in front of dominant feeling, 2 for next and 3 for next.)

    _____ Much liking, warmth, supportiveness

    _____ Much withdrawal, and irrelevant discussion

    _____ Much conflict, antagonism, attacking

    _____ Much dependence on instructor, rules, past plans

13. Group conduct

everyone spoke to whole group	some pairing	everyone spoke only to his immediate neighbor

14. What should we do next?

11. MID-YEAR REPORT OF ORIENTATION COUN-
SELORS

DATE _____

STUDENT _____   ORIENTATION COUNSELOR _____

1. With regard to academic achievement, my counselee seems
   ( ) to be achieving above what his intellectual capacity
        would indicate
   ( ) to be achieving to the maximum of his ability
   ( ) to be achieving almost up to his ability
   ( ) to be inconsistent in his achievement
   ( ) not to be achieving to the maximum of his ability

2. What do you consider this student's academic potential to be
   in comparison with the college population:

   Excellent   Fair   Average   Poor   Not College
                                                   Level

3. Do you know of factors that operate to limit the student's
   achievement?
   ( ) in wrong program   ( ) poor scholastic prepara-
   ( ) indecision about   tion
        major   ( ) vocational
   ( ) inadequate study   ( ) other (please list)
        methods

4. If he is doing failing work—under what circumstances would
   you recommend continuance or dismissal?

5. With regard to personal-social problems, I would say the
   student had the following problems which interfered with
   academic progress:
   ( ) slight   ( ) moderate   ( ) great degree
        degree   degree

Problems of:

( ) health (physical)

( ) finances

( ) morals and religion

( ) home and family

( ) inability to meet emergencies or "stress" conditions

( ) social and recreational activities

( ) courtship, sex, marriage

( ) personality adjustment (emotional health)

( ) meeting people and making friends

Please elaborate on any of the above in the space provided below.

_____

_____

In helping the student solve these problems, what further resource would you suggest:

( ) general counseling by Dean of Students

( ) psychological counseling

( ) academic counseling

( ) tutoring

( ) vocational counseling

( ) remedial courses

( ) others (please list)

6. As for counselor-counselee relationships, I would say this counselee was:

( ) highly cooperative

( ) moderately cooperative

( ) uncooperative

( ) seemed to be appreciative of assistance

( ) seemed to be indifferent to assistance

( ) seemed to resent or reject assistance

Faculty Counselor _____

12. FRESHMAN COUNSELING RECORD

Name _____ Age _____ Sex _____ Date entered Hofstra _____

Mailing Address _____ Veteran? _____ If so, under which G. I. Bill?

P.L. 346 _____ P.L. 16 _____ P.L. 550 _____ P.L. 894 _____

Vocational Objective _____ Proposed major field at College _____

Best subjects in high school _____ Poorest subjects _____

Father's present occupation _____ Father's education _____

Mother's present occupation _____ Mother's education _____

Are your parents living together? _____ Do you live with your parents? _____

Age of brother(s) _____ Age of sister(s) _____

Your marital status _____ Number of children, if any _____

Leisure time activities _____ High school activities _____

Which scholarship do you hold, if any _____ Physical limitations, if any _____

PSYCHOLOGICAL TEST RESULTS

Test	Natl %ile	Test	Natl %ile	Test	Natl %ile	Test	Natl %ile
A.C.E.		*3. Eff. of Exp.*		*C.E.E.B.*		Elementary	
Q		*Kuder*		V		Algebra	
L		Out		M			
T		Mech				Social	
		Comp				Studies	
Coop. English Tests		Sci		*IQ Results*			
1. Reading Comp		Pers		Test Date IQ		Natural	
Vocab		Art				Sciences	
Speed		Lit					
Comp		Mus				Engineering & Physical	
Total Score		Soc Serv				Science Aptitude	
2. Mechs. of Exp.		Cler					

Name _____

Dates Interviewed	Data Obtained

FRESHMAN STUDY PROGRAM

Scheduling Notes:

1st sem.

Course	Days	Hours	Credits	Mid-term Grade	Final Grade

Cumulative average end of 1st sem. _____

2nd sem.

Extra-curricular activities at Hofstra:

Extra-curricular interests not provided for at Hofstra:

Part-time job held, if any _____

Number of hours working per week _____

Interview appointments not kept _____

13. SYNOPSIS OF TOPICS FOR ORIENTATION CLASS

The Orientation course deals with some of the experiences that will face you as a college student. Some of them are broad and intangible, like problems of human relations; others are more limited and practical, like study techniques and the use of the library. Some of them can be studied, discussed, and solved in a short time; others will take considerable time and effort.

The topics that are commonly discussed in Orientation classes are listed below. You need not feel limited, however, to these alone, nor feel obliged to take them up in the order given. You are free to bring up for discussion anything that gives you real concern, and you are free to say exactly what you feel and think on any topic that comes up.

The text for Orientation is CONTROVERSY, by Hoffmann and Plutchik. In addition we recommend "How to Study," by Thomas F. Staton, or any other good how-to-study book.

Topics for Study and Discussion

1. What Should College Do For the Individual? (Section 1)
2. What is Meant by a Liberal Education? (Section 1)
3. Academic Skills and Techniques (Section 2 and Staton)
   a. Study habits and study conditions
   b. The use of the Library
   c. Preparing for and taking examinations
   d. How to take notes
4. The Nature and Function of Co-curricular Activities (Section 1)

5. Co-curricular Activities at Hofstra
6. Student-Teacher Relationships (Section 3)
    a. What should we expect?
    b. What should be expected of us?
7. Student-Parent Relationships (Section 7)
    a. Where do the parents fit in the Educational picture?
    b. The struggle toward independence
8. Prejudice (Section 6)
    a. What is it?
    b. Where is it?
    c. What are its origins?
    d. Is there a cure?
9. The Democratic Process in Human Relations (Section 6, Section 3)
    a. Its essence
    b. Its aim
    c. Its faults
10. Authoritarianism in Human Relations (Section 3, Section 7, Section 6)
    a. Its essence
    b. Its aims (and origins)
    c. Its faults
11. Morality (Section 3, Section 4)
    a. Can it be legislated?
    b. Is it necessary?
    c. Campus applications: cheating, drinking and sex
12. Social Competence (manners, dress, speech) (Section 5, Section 4)
    a. Reasons
    b. Uses
13. Personal Goals (Section 5, Section 8)
    a. What can I give to life?

      b. What can life give to me?

      c. What is my vocational future?

14. Today's World (Section 8)

      a. The age of the atom

      b. Possibility of a united world

1. Listed after most of the topics above are the Section numbers in CONTROVERSY that deal with the topic. Your reading in the text is supposed to give you intellectual ammunition for your class discussion. You will be using the readings to support the opinions and ideas put forward in class. The Sections listed after the topics are not necessarily the *only* ones that deal with the topic.

2. There will be a departmental final examination. It will not ask you specific questions on the readings but will require you to bring your knowledge of the readings to the support of your answers. For example, you will *not* be asked specific questions on "Rumblings in the Fraternities," by Morris Kaplan; but you may well be asked to describe shortcomings of fraternities, and to do so you would be expected to draw on Kaplan's article and two or three others in order to support your statements. The more thoroughly and the more broadly you read in CONTRO-VERSY the more likely you are to do well in the class discussions and the final exam. You should beware, however, of leaning so heavily on the readings that you weaken your own ability for original thinking.

3. The emphasis is on group action and discussion rather than on lecture. Your instructor will lead your discussion and may introduce you to certain devices commonly used by small discussion groups. (For example, buzz sessions, role playing, and panel presentations.) It will be up to you, however, to search out and supply the information necessary to develop and validate your discussion.

4. Your instructor will also be your personal counselor. He will arrange for periodic conferences with each individual in the class during which you are free to discuss your personal problems, large or small.

5. The seating arrangement is usually circular in order to facilitate discussion, and name cards are used so that we can get well acquainted as quickly as possible.

6. Aside from the differences noted above, we operate within the same framework and within the same limits as other classes in the College. Attendance regulations, grades, and smoking rules all apply in the same manner to Orientation as they do to other courses.

7. What you get out of Orientation depends largely on you. You are expected to contribute to your own self development and to the development of others in the group by studying and discussing the problems listed and by helping in every way that you can to make the group productive for everyone. The course is not intended to do things for you but to help you do things for yourself.

Index